Passing the Mantle

Generation to Generation

Passing the Mantle

Generation to Generation

BY

JOY HANEY

AND GUEST WRITERS:
NONA FREEMAN
ELSIE LUND
VESTA MANGUN
NILAH MEAN
BOBBYE WENDELL

WORD AFLAME PRESS

PASSING THE MANTLE

by Joy Haney

Cover design by Ben Meydam

Printed in the United States of America

Printed by

WORD AFLAME PRESS
8855 Dunn Road, Hazelwood, MO 63042
www.pentecostalpublishing.com

Library of Congress Cataloging-in-Publication Data

Haney, Joy, 1942-
Passing the mantle : generation to generation / by Joy Haney and guest writers, Nona Freeman . . . [et al.].
p. cm.
Includes bibliographical references.
ISBN-13: 978-1-56722-700-0
1. Christian women—Religious life. 2. Discipling (Christianity) I. Title.
BV4527
248.8'43—dc22 2006025517

Table of Contents

Foreword 7

Acknowledgments 9

Introduction 11

1. Passing the Mantle 13
   Joy Haney, Nona Freeman
2. Mantle of Prayer 19
   Joy Haney, Vesta Mangun
3. Mantle of Fasting 47
   Joy Haney
4. Mantle of Sacrifice 59
   Bobbye Wendell
5. Mantle of Hunger 73
   Joy Haney
6. Mantle of Truth 87
   Joy Haney
7. Mantle of Holiness 103
   Joy Haney
8. Mantle of Faith 113
   Joy Haney
9. Mantle of Faithfulness 129
   Joy Haney, Nilah Mean
10. Mantle of Character 155
    Joy Haney
11. Mantle of Love 173
    Joy Haney

12. Mantle of the Supernatural 181
Joy Haney, Elsie Lund
Epilogue 197
Guest Authors' Bios 199
Notes 207

FOREWORD

It is God's desire to preserve significant and important truths, and passing something from one generation to another is substantiated in the following verses of Scriptures:

PRAISE:

Psalm 145:1-4: "I will extol thee, my God, O king; and I will bless thy name for ever and ever. Every day will I bless thee; and I will praise thy name for ever and ever. Great is the LORD, and greatly to be praised; and his greatness is unsearchable. One generation shall praise thy works to another, and shall declare thy mighty acts."

Psalm 79:13: "So we thy people and sheep of thy pasture will give thee thanks for ever: we will shew forth thy praise to all generations."

WORD:

Psalm 12:6-7: "The words of the LORD are pure words: as silver tried in a furnace of earth, purified seven times. Thou shalt keep them, O LORD, thou shalt preserve them from this generation for ever."

NAME:

Psalm 45:17: "I will make thy name to be remembered in all generations: therefore shall the people praise thee for ever and ever."

Exodus 3:14-15: "And God said unto Moses, I AM THAT I AM: and he said, Thus shalt thou say unto the children of Israel, I AM hath sent me unto you. And God said moreover unto Moses, Thus shalt thou say unto the children of Israel, The LORD God of your fathers, the God of Abraham, the God of Issac, and the God of Jacob, hath sent me unto you: this is my name for ever, and this is my memorial unto all generations."

TRUTH:

Psalm 100:5: "For the LORD is good; his mercy is everlasting; and his truth endureth to all generations."

SALVATION:

Isaiah 51:8: "My righteousness shall be for ever, and my salvation from generation to generation."

EVERLASTING KINGDOM:

Daniel 4:3: "How great are his signs! And how mighty are his wonders! his kingdom is an everlasting kingdom, and his dominion is from generation to generation."

HIS MERCY:

Luke 1:50: "And his mercy is on them that fear him from generation to generation."

Acknowledgments

Special praise is due and given to the Lord Jesus Christ for His inspiration and anointing.

Thanks to the following people for helping to make this book happen:

Robert Fuller for his valuable work as editor in chief

Margie McNall for her excellent help and oversight of the production of this project

Joy Hudspeth for helping collect bios and pictures of the guest writers

Sue Jackson for her help in contacting the guest writers

Jina Crain for her help as production manager

Ben Meydam for his talented work in creating a beautiful cover

Bethany Sledge for her excellent proofreading

Barbara Kellar for sharing her thoughts about *passing the mantle* in an email

All the wonderful workers in the publishing department

The five guest writers not only for their spiritual insight, but for their life: Nona Freeman, Elsie Lund, Vesta Mangun, Nilah Mean, and Bobbye Wendell.

Introduction

In August 2005, while in prayer the Lord gave me inspiration to have a "Passing the Mantle" service at Ladies' Day General Conference 2006. I did not share this with anyone but only prayed and waited until the right time to share it.

My first official meeting concerning this was with Phyllis Jones and Sue Jackson. We met the first of March 2006, during the General Board sessions, and they were excited about it.

Sister Jones contacted Delissa Cox about having the Dorcas sewing group from Louisiana make the mantles for us. We needed one thousand mantles, and we wanted them to be beautiful. They agreed and were very eager to do it. They all said that the mantles had to be special—that they would be heirlooms to pass from generation to generation.

The way we planned it to happen was that the younger ministers' wives, ages forty and under, would sit in a special section, and the older ministers' wives would sit in another special section. Since then we have also added lady ministers and missionaries who are not married.

At the appointed time, the young ladies in ministry would make a circle around the building single file, and then the older ladies in ministry would go stand in front of each of them. At the same time, they would all wrap the mantles around the shoulders of the younger ones and then pray one mighty prayer together, passing on the mantle of anointing and all that it symbolized.

The more I prayed, it seemed that the Lord impressed me one service was not enough, that we needed to put a book into their hands addressing the different mantles. I felt impressed to ask five older women, soldiers of the cross, all great soulwinners, who have given their entire lives to help spread the gospel of Jesus Christ. These mighty prayer warriors and humble servants of the cross are as follows:

Nona Freeman, missionary, who is ninety years old this year;

Elsie Lund, retired missionary of over forty years;

Vesta Mangun, pastor's wife, speaker, recording artist, and author;

Nilah Mean, senior pastor of the Pentecostal Church in Dartmouth, Nova Scotia, Canada;

Bobbye Wendell, retired missionary and currently speaker at Ladies Conferences.

Here is a book that is written from the heart, filled with life's experiences, and anointed by God. May it be a blessing to each of you who read it!

1

Passing the Mantle

BY JOY HANEY AND NONA FREEMAN

JOY HANEY

The passing of the mantle is important to insure that the truths, doctrines, and the message of Jesus Christ do not die, nor are they allowed to become less effective. The miracles, signs, and wonders must continue, even escalate based on a solid foundation of the Word.

The mantle stands for the **M**essage, **A**ttitudes, the **N**ame of Jesus, **T**ruth, **L**ove, and **E**ternal values. It is something that is intangible and cannot be handled with physical hands. It is caught in the Spirit with spiritual hands. When Elijah let go of his mantle as he was taken away into the heavens, Elisha reached out and caught the mantle that came floating down to him.

In this generation of younger ladies in God's service there is a reaching out with your hands for deeper things of the Spirit. You hunger for more of God and sometimes wonder how to attain it. This book will let you glimpse into the lives of those who have walked before you. May you learn from the words contained in this book—the stories, experiences, and the Word that is shared—may you be inspired, challenged, enlightened, and find guidance.

Recently I read a handwritten letter that my mother had written to me while she lay on her deathbed. I treasure this letter. It had been quite awhile since I had read it, but as I read it, I noticed she was passing the things to me that really mattered. She wrote about my faith, my cheerful spirit, my walk with God, my involvement in His work, my role as a pastor's wife, and my role as a mother. She didn't mention my clothes, house, car, or physical looks, but she complimented me on virtues and things of the heart. She asked me to help keep the family together after she was gone, and she reminded me of things we had talked about that were important to her. She was passing the mantle of responsibility to me. She trusted me to do what was right.

My mother was a godly woman and always served the Lord with all her heart. She made sure her children went to church, prayed every day, had good character, and in general walked in God's ways. As she passed this heritage on to me, I have done my best to pass it on to our children.

That is what this book is about. It is not about how much money you will acquire in life, the name-brand clothes, the fancy homes, and all the baggage that you accumulate with each passing year. It is about what you do for Christ with your life. "Only what's done for Christ will last" is really true.

In July 2006, I received the following email letter from Barbara Keller, pastor's wife in Ohio. This is a confirmation that God has ordained this service at General Conference 2006:

"Just wanted to let you know that Debbie Saiz and I sat at North American Youth Congress in Atlanta, Georgia, over lunch about four years ago and talked about the mantle

(Debbie and I grew up together in Louisiana). We talked about whether or not we would be able *and* willing *to handle the responsibility that came along with the mantle that our grandparents and parents would be passing down to us.*

"When I returned home from Congress, a man came up to me after our Sunday morning service who would have had no idea what I was considering (the mantle) and prophesied to me that I was to do what the Lord had been talking to me about. Then he blurted it out and said to me, 'You are to take the mantle that has been passed down to you from your grandparents and your parents, and God will help you with the responsibility that comes with accepting it.'

"I could not believe it! He was the most unassuming person whom God used to come to tell me this. I really did not even know him. He said that the Lord showed him this through his prayer time.

"Wow! So a few years later (thought I was going to be one of the young ones . . . Ha!) but now that I am forty-six, I guess I will be the one passing it on. It is wonderful to know that this is what God has placed on your heart for this service.

"My daughter has always said, 'Lord, help me to be able to handle the responsibility that comes with the talent that you have given to me.'

"I am saying today, 'Lord, help me to be able to handle the responsibility that comes with the mantle *that You have placed upon me.'"*

NONA FREEMAN

The moving of the prophetic ministry in Elijah sent him to search for his follow-up. He found him plowing with twelve yoke of oxen. No doubt Elisha had a longing to do something for God and to be *somebody* in God's scheme of events, but he did not fold his hands and idly wait for God to speak or give directions—he did something profitable while he waited. Too many folks sit idly waiting for God's call. He usually calls "busy" people.

Elijah was led to Elisha where he plowed and flung his mantle over him without a word. That brings up another point; when the call does come, what is next? The Word only offers us clues. He honored his parents with a proper farewell, offered his sacrifice, and *went after Elijah, ministering unto him*. They made a good team!

This following beautiful, accurate story is found in II Kings 2:1-14. The prophets Elijah and Elisha were making one of their usual rounds—this one started in Gilgal. While there Elijah knew that his departure was soon to be. He told Elisha, "You stay here, for God is sending me to Bethel." Elisha answered, "As the LORD liveth, and as thy soul liveth, I will not leave thee." So they went to Bethel together.

While in Bethel, again Elijah said, "Stay." And Elisha refused. There is another lesson to be learned here. A voice will say, "Park here!" This is a remarkable clue for would-be mantle-holders. Watch where you park! While it is human to want to rest in a comfortable place—it may not be the will of God. If you ever inherit a mantle, you will have to discern when and where to park and when it is the will of God to keep moving.

The sons of the prophets at Jericho reiterated what those at Bethel had said, "Knowest thou that the LORD will take away thy master from thee?" but Elisha repeated the same answer to them, "Yea, I know it; hold ye your peace."

Then his leader Elijah said to him, "Tarry, I pray thee, here; for the LORD hath sent me to Jordan." Again Elisha refused to stay behind and answered, "As the LORD liveth, and as thy soul liveth, I will not leave thee." Many people will join with the fifty prophets standing to view from afar, but only those who tenaciously stay close to Jesus will see the miracles.

The prophet of the Lord and his protégé stood by the bank of the Jordan. Suddenly, Elijah wrapped his mantle together and smote the waters so they divided and they too went over on dry ground. Elijah then asked Elisha what he could do for him before he was taken away. Elisha said it exactly: *let a double portion of thy spirit be upon me.* Elijah told him he had asked a hard thing, "but if you see me when I am taken, it shall be so; but if not, it shall not be so."

As they went on talking, suddenly a chariot of fire and horses of fire separated the friends and Elijah went to heaven by a whirlwind. What an awesome experience! This has never happened before or since. Elisha was a brave man, and he knew what he wanted. He asked and received it.

Since Elisha did see him go, Elisha did something very significant—he tore his clothes into two pieces, took up the mantle that fell from Elijah as he ascended, and returned to Jordan.

The proof came as he came back to Jordan. He took Elijah's mantle that fell from him, rolled it up and hit the waters and shouted, "Where is the LORD God of Elijah? and when he also had smitten the waters, they parted hither and thither: and Elisha went over."

Serious Bible scholars have determined that Elisha actually did twice the number of miracles that Elijah did, lacking one. After Elijah's fifty years of successful ministry under four kings: Jehoram, Jehu, Jehoahaz, and Joash, God had a unique plan for an amazing postscript to his life!

> *And it came to pass, as they were burying a man, that, behold, they spied a band of men; and they cast the man into the sepulchre of Elisha: and when the man was let down, and touched the bones of Elisha, he revived, and stood up on his feet* (II Kings 13:21).

Wow! Though the Bible tells us nothing further about the man, when he touched the bones of the dead prophet, the dead man stood on his feet and lived! The point is made, promised by God, double means double.

Since the Scriptures give us lessons that we should act upon—nothing is recorded that does not bring us profit—this is a lesson that we can follow today. The precious older brothers and sisters in the Lord who have learned to follow through on the miraculous can pass their mantle to the younger generation who seek to know more about the moving of the Spirit.

I recently attended the farewell service for our dear friend, T. W. Barnes. That meeting had an unusual anointing on it, and in prayer the previous night, Jesus spoke to me to rejoice in the beautiful life of a prophet who had faithfully declared the Word given him. He also said that He would put the mantle of Tom Barnes on the humble and willing. Hebrews 13:8 declares, "Jesus Christ the same yesterday, and to day, and for ever."

2

Mantle of Prayer

BY JOY HANEY AND VESTA MANGUN

JOY HANEY

Nothing brings more fragrance into the life of an individual than the simple act of prayer. To be in the presence of God brings joy, relief from pressures, and much needed answers as stated in Psalm 16:11: "Thou wilt shew me the path of life: in thy presence is fulness of joy; at thy right hand there are pleasures for evermore."

Prayer is the lifeline of a Christian. Without it, there is spiritual death. Nothing compares to its power. Oh, may women everywhere pray much in these last days! It is a force that conquers hell and its envoys. This is the need of the hour, and we must use it for the change and transformation of impossible situations as expressed in the following paragraph:

> Prayer is the greatest force we can wield. It is the greatest talent God has given. He has given it to every Christian. What right have we to leave unappropriated or unapplied the

greatest force which God has ordained for the salvation and transformation of men?

—JOHN R. MOTT[1]

To think that God, the exalted One, would allow common man to enter into His presence and talk with Him in common everyday language is beyond understanding. In my lifetime I have seen Him, high and lifted up (not as Isaiah described his encounter with God), but this year the greatness of His majesty is pulsating within me as never before.

> *In the year that king Uzziah died I saw also the Lord sitting upon a throne, high and lifted up, and his train filled the temple. Above it stood the seraphims: each one had six wings; with twain he covered his face, and with twain he covered his feet, and with twain he did fly. And one cried unto another, and said, Holy, holy, holy, is the* LORD *of hosts: the whole earth is full of his glory* (Isaiah 6:1-3).

A SECRET PLACE

The greatest thing you can do, whether as a minister's wife, a lady minister, lady missionary, or a human being, is to find a place where you can pray and talk to God, for you will need Him every day, sometimes more desperately than others. You need a place where you can shut yourself in, if even for a few minutes, where it is just you and Jesus. This is as important as natural breathing, for prayer is spiritual breathing.

S. Chrysotom wrote:

> Prayer is the medicine expelling spiritual sickness, the foundation of the spiritual building,

> that which the soul is to the body. The man [woman] without prayer is as the fish out of water, and gasping for life, as a city without walls, and open to all attacks; but from him that is armed with prayer the tempter starts back, as midnight robbers start back when they see a sword suspended over a soldier's bed.[2]

This morning when I entered into my place of prayer, I began to sing that old song:

> Shut in with God in a secret place,
> There in the Spirit beholding His face.
> Gaining new power to run in this race,
> I long to be shut in with God!

The second time I sang it, I changed the word "long" to "love."

> Shut in with God in a secret place,
> There in the Spirit beholding His face.
> Gaining new power to run in this race,
> I love to be shut in with God!

As I began to approach His throne and talk to Him, I felt the presence of Jesus, and as I wept before Him, I felt the cares of life slip away from me and I began to ascend into a place of utter peace and joy that only comes from touching Him.

There is no greater place to be than in His presence. You can tell Him all things, and He understands. Not only does He come, but He also gives a peace concerning the things that trouble your mind. He wraps you in the warmth of His love and lifts you into the realm of faith and glory. He alone has all power in heaven and in earth, and it is His good pleasure to help His children.

Another time this week, I had to drive thirty miles to get to my destination, and on the way I began to sing the word, *Glory*, over and over as praise to Him. Immediately the presence of the Lord filled the car so strong and I went from singing *glory* to singing *Hallelujah*! Glory filled my soul as I communed in worship to Jesus, with tears washing my eyes as I spoke in tongues, driving down the highway. It seemed as if the thirty minutes were just a few minutes. And the same thing happened on the way back home. It reminded me once more that communication with God can be anyplace, anytime, by anyone. Secret places can be wherever you are if you shut everything else from your mind.

Psalm 91:1 promises that we can be in very close proximity to God if we desire to be: "He that dwelleth in the secret place of the most High shall abide under the shadow of the Almighty."

Hosea 14:7 expresses what happens when we abide under His shadow: "They that dwell under his shadow shall return; they shall revive as the corn, and grow as the vine."

It is a secret place of power! When hell turns up the heat, get under the shadow. The power of this shadow is described in Isaiah:

> *O Lord, thou art my God; I will exalt thee, I will praise thy name; for thou hast done wonderful things; thy counsels of old are faithfulness and truth. . . . For thou hast been a strength to the poor, a strength to the needy in his distress, a refuge from the storm, a shadow from the heat, when the blast of the terrible ones is as a storm against the wall* (Isaiah 25:1, 4).

Prayer can be a place to escape from the hot fires of life or from the responsibilities that weigh heavily upon your mind and the demanding schedules that nudge you relentlessly as a robber nudges his victim in the back with a gun.

Isaiah 26:20 says it well: "Come, my people, enter thou into thy chambers, and shut thy doors about thee: hide thyself as it were for a little moment."

It is important to have those places of being hidden with God, as the song says, "Rock of ages, cleft for me, Let me hide myself in Thee."

Find a place where you can be alone with God and follow the instructions of Psalm 100:4: "Enter into his gates with thanksgiving, and into his courts with praise: be thankful unto him, and bless his name."

Prayer and praise should always be together. This is proven in Acts 16:25 when Paul and Silas were thrown into prison after they had been beaten: "And at midnight Paul and Silas prayed, and sang praises unto God: and the prisoners heard them." The results were that God sent an earthquake and they were loosed from their bonds.

Those who pray only, without praising God in faith, will find they are still sad. After you pray earnestly, then you need to leave your requests with God and begin to praise Him, for He inhabits the praises of His people. If not immediately, you should soon feel the presence of God flood your soul. There will come a lightening of the load and a refreshment of the spirit. Once more you know that "all is well," because you have just been touched by divinity.

In the 1800s, Charles Haddon Spurgeon was England's best-known preacher for most of the nineteenth century. He wrote the following paragraphs about "private prayers" that need to be inserted here:

Keep the altar of private prayer burning. This is the very life of all piety. The sanctuary and family altars borrow their fires here; therefore let this burn well. Secret devotion is the very essence, evidence, and barometer of vital and experimental religion.

Burn here the fat of your sacrifices. Let your closet seasons be, if possible, regular, frequent, and undisturbed. Effectual prayer availeth much.

Let us examine ourselves on this important matter. Do we engage with lukewarmness in private devotion? Is the fire of devotion burning dimly in our hearts? Do the chariot wheels drag heavily? If so, let us be alarmed at this sign of decay. Let us go with weeping, and ask for the Spirit of grace and of supplication.

HOW DO I DO THIS?

As a young minister's wife with young children, sometimes you feel torn between meeting the many needs of the children, the housework, the work of the ministry, and just life itself. As you hear the older women talk about secret places of prayer, daily prayer, and getting alone with God, you sometimes feel guilty because you cannot have this perfect schedule and you end up feeling frazzled and frustrated.

If you truly want to develop a consistent walk with God and are seeking the things of God even in the midst of potty training, nursing feverish brows, and fixing school lunches, I want to take the guilt from you.

There are ways to do this. We are told consistently in the Bible to pray without ceasing, pray continually, and to pray always.

> *As for me, I will call upon God; and the* LORD *shall save me. Evening, and morning, and at noon, will I pray, and cry aloud: and he shall hear my voice* (Psalm 55:16-17).

This is pretty much an all-day thing.

Jesus talked about praying every day in the Lord's Prayer.

> *Our Father which art in heaven, Hallowed be thy name. Thy kingdom come. Thy will be done in earth, as it is in heaven. Give us this day our daily bread* (Matthew 6:9).

It was a *daily* thing.

Luke 18:1: "Men ought always to pray, and not to faint." *Always* is consistent and forever!

Paul addressed this "always" praying in Ephesians 6:18: "Praying always with all prayer and supplication in the Spirit, and watching thereunto with all perseverance and supplication for all saints."

I Thessalonians 5:17 commands: "Pray without ceasing."

The disciples put prayer on their daily schedule. This is demonstrated in Acts 3:1: "Now Peter and John went up together into the temple at the hour of prayer, being the ninth hour."

God listens for our prayers. It is important to Him as revealed in I Peter 3:12: "For the eyes of the Lord are over the righteous, and his ears are open unto their prayers."

I Peter 4:7 admonishes us to pray: "But the end of all things is at hand: be ye therefore sober, and watch unto prayer." *Watch unto prayer* is being alert and giving time to staying in communication with God.

Paul instructed in Romans 12:12: "Continuing instant in prayer." This refers to having a spirit of prayer, that at any given moment you can touch God. This comes from having daily communication with Him. This is what prayer is.

David gave the morning as his time of prayer: "My voice shalt thou hear in the morning, O LORD; in the morning will I direct my prayer unto thee, and will look up" (Psalm 5:3).

It is established that we should have daily prayers, so how do you do it? First of all, prayer should be looked upon as a privilege of being able to talk to God. It should not be viewed with the attitude of, "I have to pray." It should be, "I can't wait to talk to God."

I have developed a lifestyle of continually talking to God. This is what was meant by *praying without ceasing*. You bring God into your life by talking to Him about everything. It doesn't matter what it is; learn to talk to God about it, even if you are not on your knees. When you are frustrated about something, talk to God about it. When you need something and don't know where to find it, pray, and don't forget to add praise to that prayer *before* and *after* He helps you find it.

But what are some practical ways of finding that secret place that is so needed for the soul?

When we lived in the St. Louis, Missouri, area in 1970, our fourth child was born. We had two babies at the same time, thirteen months apart. Needless to say, I was a full-time mom and did not do any speaking or travel much with my husband (he was the UPC National Youth President at the time).

I was not out front in the limelight, and that was not important to me. In fact, I didn't even think about it. All that mattered to me was that I was a good wife and mother. I cared much about my children and spent my waking hours with them.

At the same time, I also had a fervent desire for the things of God. I had been raised in a home that put much emphasis on prayer and had seen it demonstrated in our home, so it was a natural thing for me to want to continue in a practice that seemed to bring so much power and blessing.

How did I do this with a newborn and a thirteen-month-old, both in diapers? I didn't read in a book how to do it; my great love for Jesus and wanting to be with Him dictated to me what to do.

I remember getting the other two children off to school, then taking care of the two babies, dressing and feeding them. Then I would take them downstairs to the playroom, and there I would kneel and pray. The baby would be in her special car seat, and the toddler would be playing with her toys. Many were the times when she would play *horsey* on my back, and say, "Mommy cry." And I would hug and kiss her and say, "Mommy is talking to Jesus," and she would cuddle with me for a moment and then go about playing with her toys.

When we were in Stockton before the move to Missouri, and after we moved back, for the most part my *secret place* of prayer was in the morning before the children awakened. This was not difficult for me because I had been raised to get up at 6:00 every morning of my life while growing up as a child. So it seemed the natural thing to do to get up and pray while the day was fresh, the birds were singing, the dew was on the grass. It was quiet and still. There were no phones ringing, no one knocking at the door, just peace before the rush of the day began.

Another of my favorite places to pray when I was a young minister's wife was in the bathtub while taking a bath. As I cleansed my body, I took a spiritual bath and let the Holy Spirit wash my frustrations away. I have always found that when I give all my troubles and loads to Jesus, it lifts my spirit and brings a song back into my heart. When I keep it all bottled up inside of me, there is a heaviness that weighs upon me. Prayer is a release, as Jesus instructed in Matthew 11:28: "Come unto me, all ye that labour and are heavy laden, and I will give you rest."

I believe that prayer should be as natural to us as breathing. We should learn to talk to Jesus while driving in the car, while getting dressed, while walking through the house, cooking, cleaning, nursing, working, or whatever we are doing; there should be an awareness of Him. *In our hearts* we should always be sitting at His feet, wanting to be near Him, to learn of Him, just as Mary did in Luke 10:39: "And she had a sister called Mary, which also sat at Jesus' feet, and heard his word."

What did Jesus say about this? Luke 10:42 says that He applauded her: "But one thing is needful: and Mary hath chosen that good part, which shall not be taken away from her."

No task, no one, or nothing should be allowed to take away that relationship you have with Jesus. It is the most glorious experience in the world to be on daily talking terms with the exalted One, King of kings, Lord of lords, everlasting Father, the one true God: Jesus. Take advantage of this privilege and bring Him into your daily lifestyle. He wants to be the center of your life and to sit on the throne of your heart.

Jesus does not want you to feel guilty because you cannot sit in perfect conditions, saying pious prayers, impressing those around you. He does not ask for that. He desires for you to have a relationship with Him where

He knows that He is important to you and that you talk to Him daily. Just make Him number one in your life and hunger for Him and His Word, and you will find yourself talking to Him and including Him in your life no matter where you are or what you're doing.

FERVENT PRAYERS

There are many kinds of prayers. There are the prayers at the dinner table, the whispered prayers before a difficult assignment, the times when we call, "Jesus," at the time of an emergency, and then there are the times when we pray with strong prayers of travail and fervency when we are driven to our knees.

Jesus taught us how to pray many times by example. One such example is recorded in Hebrews 5:7: "Who in the days of his flesh, when he had offered up prayers and supplications with strong crying and tears."

There are times when we go to pray that we cannot articulate words to express our deep emotions about a situation. That is when the Spirit prays through us in tongues and even groanings.

> *Likewise the Spirit also helpeth our infirmities: for we know not what we should pray for as we ought: but the Spirit itself maketh intercession for us with groanings which cannot be uttered* (Romans 8:26).

James 5:16 promises that fervent prayers will bring results: "The effectual fervent prayer of a righteous man availeth much." Fervent prayers are hot, glowing, burning, intense petitions to the only One who can do anything about what you are praying.

Women have many pressures. Prayer is a release from those things that bear down on you. Hannah, our beautiful friend who was the mother of Samuel, found this to be true. The day she sat at the table with her husband and the other woman who had borne him children was just one time too many. Peninnah often provoked Hannah and goaded her, until finally she could not stand it any longer. Hannah got desperate.

> *And her adversary [Peninnah] also provoked her sore, for to make her fret, because the LORD had shut up her womb. And as he did so year by year, when she went up to the house of the LORD, so she provoked her; therefore she wept, and did not eat* (I Samuel 1:6-7).

We've all been there: tears are in your heart so that you cannot eat. When this happened to Hannah, it was the thing that drove her to her knees. She rose from the table and left the place of laughter and feasting and made her way to a secret place.

"And she was in bitterness of soul, and prayed unto the LORD, and wept sore" (I Samuel 1:10). As she prayed the priest watched her, and Eli came to her and told her to quit drinking and put wine away from her. He thought she was drunk.

> *And Hannah answered and said, No, my lord, I am a woman of a sorrowful spirit: I have drunk neither wine nor strong drink, but have poured out my soul before the LORD* (I Samuel 1:15).

This was strong, fervent praying, and God answered her by prophesying through the priest: "Then Eli answered and said, Go in peace: and the God of Israel grant thee thy petition that thou hast asked of him" (I Samuel 1:17).

How many prayers had Hannah prayed? How many times had her heart been broken? It is unclear in the Scriptures, but it does say that Peninnah had sons and daughters, and that takes years to happen.

The good thing is that God finally answered her prayer, and that particular day she left the temple she was sad no more. She had heard from God and she left happy: "And she said, Let thine handmaid find grace in thy sight. So the woman went her way, and did eat, and her countenance was no more sad" (I Samuel 1:18).

One year later, she gave birth to a baby boy and she named him Samuel, "because I have asked him of the LORD" (I Samuel 1:20). He became a great man who walked with God and became God's prophet and priest who influenced many for righteousness. What if Hannah had not prayed her fervent prayer?

PRAYERS OF FAITH

Jude 1:20 instructs us to build up our faith by praying in the Holy Ghost: "But ye, beloved, building up yourselves on your most holy faith, praying in the Holy Ghost." Praying in the Holy Ghost is letting the Spirit pray through you in unknown tongues.

Believe when you pray, as instructed in Mark 11:24, and He will answer your prayers: "Therefore I say unto you, What things soever ye desire, when ye pray, believe that ye receive them, and ye shall have them."

He does not always answer immediately, but keep praying and believing because prayers never die! The day will come when your accumulated prayers will come up before Him as strong incense that cannot be ignored. That is when He will begin to move in your behalf.

God is constantly searching the earth, wanting to work strongly in behalf of those who seek Him.

> *For the eyes of the* LORD *run to and fro throughout the whole earth, to shew himself strong in the behalf of them whose heart is perfect toward him* (II Chronicles 16:9).

That means that you are not divided in your affections toward Him. He is the Lord of your life, and your faith and confidence are in Him.

During one ladies' retreat, the Lord spoke this to me several years ago, but the message is still the same: "I have seen your tears. I have heard your groanings. Know this: that I am with you. Because of your prayers you have placed yourself near my heart. Continue to stay close to me and I will lead you into places you've never been. My eyes search the earth daily for those who would spend time with me. Remember you are the apple of my eye and I love you. Your prayers are recorded in heaven and they will be answered according to my plan."

This is proven in the story of Zacharias and Elisabeth. "And they were both righteous before God, walking in all the commandments and ordinances of the Lord blameless" (Luke 1:6).

They wanted a son and prayed to God for this to happen. One day while Zacharias was doing his duties as a priest, an angel appeared unto him, which said to him:

> *Fear not, Zacharias: for thy prayer is heard; and thy wife Elisabeth shall bear thee a son, and thou shalt call his name John* (Luke 1:13).

IMPORTANCE OF PRAYING TOGETHER

As important as it is to have a secret place of prayer for private prayers, it is important also for the church to pray together collectively.

Jesus said in Matthew 18:19: "Again I say unto you, That if two of you shall agree on earth as touching any thing that they shall ask, it shall be done for them of my Father which is in heaven."

The Book of Acts demonstrates the practice of praying together many times, as shown in some of the following instances:

Acts 1:14: "These all continued with one accord in prayer and supplication, with the women."

Acts 2:42: "And they continued stedfastly in the apostles' doctrine and fellowship, and in breaking of bread, and in prayers."

Acts 3:1: "Now Peter and John went up together into the temple at the hour of prayer."

Acts 4:31: "And when they had prayed, the place was shaken where they were assembled together."

Acts 6:4: "But we will give ourselves continually to prayer."

Acts 6:6: "And when they had prayed, they laid their hands on them."

Acts 8:15: "Who, when they were come down, prayed for them."

Acts 12:5: "Prayer was made without ceasing of the church unto God for him." *Verse 12*: "He came to the house of Mary the mother of John, whose surname was Mark; where many were gathered together praying."

The church must never stop praying. Fervent prayers will be answered, but we must pray, pray, and pray some more. Prayer is the communication between God and man. It is the simple act of humbling oneself before the mighty throne of God, asking for mercy, grace, and help in the time of need.

Prayer demands no special eloquence;
Prayer seeks no applause.
Prayer is birthed in time, but it grasps eternity;
Prayer touches the power of the world to come.

When we pray daily fervent prayers, our churches will be known as healing centers! Our people will be walking dynamos of power! This is the finest hour of the church! We will not fail but will accept the challenge and pray, pray, pray until we are filled with the Spirit every day, living and expecting miracles anywhere at anytime!

PASSING THE MANTLE: THE IMPORTANCE OF PRAYER, FASTING, AND SACRIFICE

VESTA MANGUN

Life is like a relay race, where the baton of values, character, and faith is passed from one generation to another. The runner ahead passes it on and runs by our side for a while; then we pass it on to those who come after us, one by one.

In recent years, I have come to learn at a profoundly deeper level the significant importance of passing on the apostolic mantle and spiritual inheritance of prayer, fasting, and sacrifice . . . an inheritance freely given us by those who paid a tremendous and often difficult price for what they bequeathed.

In like manner, as recipients, we obtain our spiritual inheritance by recognizing and accepting from our spiritual forefathers . . . the apostolic mantle of prayer, fasting, and sacrifice . . . and it is imperative that we *pass it on* to the next generation. Let those behind us call us faithful!

- We cannot pass on what we do not have.
- We cannot lead others where we have not been ourselves.
- Our knowledge cannot exceed our experience.
- We dare not let the chain reaction stop with us.
- We must be first partakers . . . leading the way by precept and practice.
- We can never be a success without a successor!

No one to whom the great mediation of truth has been revealed is free to let it stop there, as long as he or she may live. Every dispensation and every generation of the past is hanging on this generation. They without us cannot be made perfect.

We must reach . . . teach . . . equip . . . edify . . . and *pass on* prayer, fasting, and sacrifice to our generation. The apostolic command is "First of all, prayer" . . . "Be thou an example" . . . "Commit to faithful men and women the ministry of reconciliation" . . . "Contend for the faith" . . . "Stir up the gift of God that is within you" . . . "If by any means I may provoke to emulation them which are my flesh and might save them!"

> Freedom is never more than one generation away from extinction. We didn't pass it to our children in the bloodstream. It must be fought for, protected, and handed on for them to do the same, or one day we will spend our sunset years telling our children and our children's children what it was once like in the United States when men were free.
>
> —Ronald Reagan

The same can be said of the things of the Spirit. We cannot pass on our spiritual legacy to our children in their bloodstream. The next generation will not acquire by osmosis the power of our spiritual heritage that comes with prayer, fasting, and sacrifice. It must be preached . . . practiced . . . and *passed on*! If we do not, we are never more than one generation removed from paganism, desertion, extinction, and total oblivion.

Don't waste it . . . neglect it . . . deny it . . . compromise it . . . bury it . . . but with prayer, fasting, and whatever sacrifice is required . . . *pass it on!*

What happens when truth is not intentionally taught to the next generation? The next generation just does not know.

The *Sydney Morning Herald* reported that on December 26, 2004, a tsunami wave in the Indian Ocean caused destruction and death in eleven countries with waves up to thirty feet in height. One-quarter of a million people perished. One-third of those were children. Tsunami waves are not unknown in that part of the world. The last major tsunami in that region occurred on June 26, 1941. In the past when the ground shook, children were always taught to run up into the hills, *except for this generation*. This time, when the water pulled back, people ran to the beach to see the shells and sea animals that had been left exposed. So instead of running away from the impending tsunami, they ran directly in its path. From that point in some areas, there was about one hour before the tsunami hit. The waves destroyed all buildings one-half mile from the shore. Destruction reached one mile inland. Walking briskly, even a child can cover a mile in about twenty minutes. But no one had told them to run away.

Strangely enough, on the island of Simeulue, which was amazingly close to the earthquake epicenter and one of the first to be hit by the tsunami, not one of the seventy thousand people on the island was killed by the waves even though 90 percent of the buildings along the coast were destroyed. One report pointed out that these islanders had emphasized traditions that stemmed from a tsunami that had hit their island in 1907: when the ground shakes, run into the hills. The secret of survival had been passed on from one generation to another.

The Bible is full of generational blessings being passed on from generation to generation.

God's covenant with Abraham was also with his "seed after him." This is reiterated five times in Genesis 17:7-10.

Elijah left Elisha with his mantle, the symbol of a miraculous relationship with God. It is significant that what Elisha saw and was taught, he caught. He wanted the mantle of power desperately, and he got it, but he failed to pass it to the succeeding generation. He took the miraculous power and anointing to his grave. It was buried with him! The amazing fulfillment of Elisha's "double portion mantle" occurred when a dead man came back to life, after being laid on Elisha's dead bones in the tomb.

As spectacular as the story is, it tells the sad account of a powerfully anointed man who was unable to pass his mantle of anointing, that was passed to him by his predecessor, Elijah, to those who followed him.

As Joshua received the "mantle of Moses," God reminded him,

> *This book of the law shall not depart out of thy mouth; but thou shalt meditate therein day and night, that thou mayest observe to do according to all that is written therein: for then thou shalt make thy way prosperous, and then thou shalt have good success* (Joshua 1:8).

We must pass it on!

I have had bequeathed to me firsthand exposure to the supernatural ministry of the gospel of Jesus Christ with prayer, fasting, and sacrifice by my godly parents and other spiritual giants. Now, for more than six decades, it has been my distinguished privilege to share the inimitable life of a stalwart champion of the apostolic faith, Gerald Mangun. A man of unceasing prayer and fasting several days a week, with one or two extended seven-day fasts every year, with nothing to eat and only water to drink . . . he has lived his life as a living sacrifice, wholly, totally, and unreservedly to Jesus Christ. Refusing to be turned aside by inconsequential and secondary things, he has successfully passed it on to his children and his children's children and hundreds of spiritual children!

- I have discovered a fulfillment in prayer that nothing else offers.
- I have experienced a joy in prayer that no other activity provides.
- I am enjoying an excitement in prayer that time does not dull and no other pursuit promises.

Of all the excitement in my wonderfully busy life, the most exciting is that of prayer. Can you even imagine the priceless privilege of meeting God in prayer?

For more than four decades I have prayed and fasted the entire day on the birthday of my son, Anthony Mangun, for the will of God in his life and his ministry. Now that Gentry, his son, was born on Anthony's birthday, the day of prayer and fasting continues with fervency!

The spiritual inheritance is the only thing that will

last. Flowers given to your children may last two weeks; clothes two years; a car ten years; a house seventy years . . . but things of the Spirit, the Scripture says, are eternal (II Peter 3:10-11).

It was David's gift to God's house (put in store) that saved the life of his descendant, Joash, years later (II Kings 11:10; II Chronicles 23:9).

According to Revelation 5:8, the prayers of God's saints are stored up in golden vials, and Revelation 8:5 says these are upon the golden altar which is before the throne!

We must grasp the apostolic mantle and our spiritual inheritance with prayer, fasting, and sacrifice and *pass it on* to the next generation to advance the kingdom of God with apostolic revival and apostolic results! Doing nothing with one's spiritual inheritance is a sure sign of eventually losing it. To merely maintain the previous generation's accomplishments and mighty works . . . spells death. We have a biblical mandate to mentor . . . to guide . . . to teach . . . to counsel . . . to coach and advise others . . . and to *pass it on* not just to our own children but to spiritual sons and daughters!

We must teach them how to spend our spiritual inheritance. Do not bury it as did the one-talent man. He simply held on to what he had been given. He did not invest it or pass it on; thus, he lost it!

It is sad to see those in this, our day, who have received a spiritual inheritance . . . a mantle of apostolic truth from their parents, but failed to grasp it and *pass it on.* We must rear spiritual children who will grasp the apostolic mantle with prayer, fasting, . . . and sacrifice.

God wants to give us a spiritual explosion, exponentially using them to take the last-day revival to a higher level . . . and *pass it on!* To do this, we must help this generation understand that although spiritual inheritance is passed on, it was paid for by prayer, fasting, . . . and sacrifice . . . and they must be willing to pay whatever price required to grasp it . . . and *pass it on*.

God said,

> *As for me, this is my covenant with them, saith the LORD; My spirit that is upon thee, and my words which I have put in thy mouth, shall not depart out of thy mouth, nor out of the mouth of thy seed, nor out of the mouth of thy seed's seed, saith the LORD, from henceforth and for ever* (Isaiah 59:21).

Thy seed shall possess the gates of the enemy!

> *For as the new heavens and the new earth, which I will make, shall remain before me, saith the LORD, so shall your seed and your name remain* (Isaiah 66:22).

The baton is now in our hands. It has been trustingly, fearfully, awesomely, prayerfully, and carefully handed to us by faithful men and women. We must not drop it! We must not fool with it! We owe a debt to the past. We owe a debt to the present. We owe a debt to the future! The perpetuation of our values from one generation to the next assures our continuation.

We are this world's last hope! If we do not get serious about organized, concerted, intercessory prayer and fasting, preaching and teaching and reaching the lost, edifying, equipping, perfecting the saints and ministers, we will lose our churches and lose our generation. The job does not belong to just the preachers; it belongs to everybody. Everyone from pastors and evangelists, from seasoned saints to the newly converted, we all have been commanded to "make disciples" . . . and *pass it on!*

I am deputized; *passing it on* is not an option—it is an obligation. It is not a choice to be considered; it is a command to be obeyed.

May I paraphrase Albert Einstein: "The (future) is a dangerous place, not because of those who do evil, but because of those who look on and do nothing."

A sense of urgency must possess us. We must *pass the mantle* of prayer, fasting, and sacrifice through teaching and example to the next generation. We must get involved in teaching the next generation a love for the truth, a call to duty. We must look for opportunities to share the wisdom and experiences of our Christian walk with them. We must start today!

Two of Satan's greatest deceptions are "It won't matter" and "You can do it later." But over and over in Scripture, God repeats urgency to do it and *do it now*, particularly when it comes to this responsibility to teach the next generation divine truths concerning the matter of salvation.

Again, I reiterate, when truths are not deliberately taught to the next generation, the next generation just does not know. Martin Luther said that it is strange that every twenty years or so God builds a new church out of little children . . . which is another way of saying that the church is always just one generation away from extinction. The Christian faith must be transmitted or it will die. We must have a thrust within the church to ensure apostolic continuity with prayer, fasting, and sacrifice.

One writer identified what he has called the "grandmother" syndrome in the church. We want to have a lot of children around yet are relieved that the responsibility for their care belongs to someone else. There is an old story about a bird that built a nest with a hole in the bottom. She liked to lay eggs but did not want the responsibility of raising children. We can be guilty in the church of falling into this condition, enjoying the youngsters around but not wanting to take the responsibility of feeding and educating, but this is not an option in the church. Augustine once said, "Without God, we cannot; without us, God will not."

As we have freely received, so we must freely give. We have an obligation to build memorials for those generations who will follow us, or vital Christian concepts will be lost forever. "When your children ask in time to come, 'What do these stones mean to you?' then you shall tell them." We must erect memorials that will remind all people of what God has been and done for us. Our responsibility does not end with our lives. It is to continue beyond them. Just as we in our lifetime are indebted to many who have gone before us, so we must provide for its continuance. As Paul instructed Timothy, "Take heed unto thyself, and unto the doctrine; continue in them: for in doing this thou shalt both save thyself, and them that hear thee" (I Timothy 4:16). When I meet Peter and Paul and all those who have gone before me, will I be able to say, "I kept the faith, I finished the course"? And when I meet my children will I be able to face them with a clear conscience and know that I passed the identical thing to them, whole and intact, undiluted, uncompromised?

God will have His church with or without us, but our descendants, our posterity, our children will not be a part of it unless we *pass the mantle* to them purposefully, urgently, with focus and extreme care.

> All that is necessary for the triumph of evil is that good men do nothing.
>
> —Edmund Burke

In his will, the American patriot Patrick Henry wrote,

> I have now disposed of all my property to my family; there is one thing more I wish I could give them, and that is the Christian religion. If they had this, and I had not given them one shilling, they would be rich; but if they had not that, and I have given them all the world, they would be poor.

Herman Melville said,

> We cannot live for ourselves alone. Our lives are connected by a thousand invisible threads, and along these sympathetic fibers, our actions run as causes and return to us as results.

We must bequeath our legacy of apostolic truth and spiritual inheritance with prayer, fasting, and sacrifice.

"A good man leaveth an inheritance to his children's children" (Proverbs 13:22).

> *That our sons may be as plants grown up in their youth; that our daughters may be as corner stones, polished after the similitude of a palace* (Psalm 144:12).

The Bible prophetically reveals to us that there will be a time when the plowman will overtake the reaper, when the vats shall overflow. In other words, the harvest will be so great we will be able to plant and harvest at the same time.

Exponential, spiritual growth, momentum, and multiplication will happen when we successfully *pass on the apostolic mantle and spiritual inheritance of prayer, fasting, and sacrifice.*

In 1948 at the Olympic Games, the French relay team was well ahead. The first two runners had been amazingly swift, but when the second runner passed the baton to the third runner, it was dropped.

What a moment of tragedy! The nation's hopes were shattered. The coaches' work went for naught. The first two runners' performances were all in vain. The fourth runner did not have a chance. The boy who dropped the baton fell down and wept.

Your family continuity is in balance. The baton of one generation's values and faith is being passed on. Don't drop the baton of apostolic succession!

THE POWER OF PRAYER

The most powerful, effective, far-reaching, influential act you can perform for another human being is that you intercede before God on his or her behalf every day. All of us should have someone praying for us. You are rich if someone knows how to talk to God and intercede for you and bring your name before God. Every child needs a father or a mother who will call his or her name before our loving, merciful, heavenly Father.

We must pray when we feel the presence of God, and we must pray when the heavens seem to be as gates locked against us. Like the needy widow in Jesus' parable, we must knock relentlessly on the door of heaven until God hears and answers. We must pray when it is convenient to pray, and we must pray when great sacrifice is required. We must pray when we are strong and when we feel that we have no strength left to pray. We must pray when we have time to pray, and we must pray when demands on our schedule seem more than we can bear, because prayer will unlock the captives, break Satan's chains, and leave hell in shambles. Prayer will break the deadlock, the stranglehold on any situation. Prayer is omnipotent. Prayer can do anything God can do, go anywhere God can go.

Nothing, absolutely nothing lies beyond the reach of God. Prayer changes things. The dynamics of God are released in response to prayer, and it will be forever true, the effectual fervent prayer of a righteous man availeth much.

So in a sweet hour of prayer, I will lay down my *why* before His cross and worship kneeling, my mind sometimes too numb for thought, my heart beyond all feeling, worshiping. I realize that in knowing Him, I don't need a "Why?" I lay my *why* before His throne of grace, and I rise and triumphantly say with Habakkuk,

> *Though the fig tree does not bud and there are no grapes on the vines, though the olive crop fails and the fields produce no food, though there are no sheep in the pen and no cattle in the stalls, yet I will rejoice in the LORD, I will be joyful in God my Savior* (Habakkuk 3:17-18, NIV).

"Delight thyself also in the LORD; and he shall give thee the desires of thine heart."

3

Mantle of Fasting

BY JOY HANEY

It has often been stated: "Fasting does not change God; it changes us." It definitely changes the one who does the fasting, but there are instances in the Bible that refute the first part of this statement.

One example of this is when Moses was speaking to the children of Israel and was reiterating some of the incidents that occurred in the journey after they left Egypt. He discussed the subject of their sin—that of creating the golden calf while he was on the mountaintop with God, who was giving him the Ten Commandments. Moses told them what God spoke to him during this time:

> *And the LORD said unto me, Arise, get thee down quickly from hence; for thy people which thou hast brought forth out of Egypt have corrupted themselves; they are quickly turned aside out of the way which I commanded them; they have made them a molten image* (Deuteronomy 9:12).

Verse 14 states what God was going to do because of this: "Let me alone, that I may destroy them, and blot out their name from under heaven: and I will make of thee a nation mightier and greater than they."

Moses continued to address the people and told them that he did come down from the mountaintop and found them worshiping the golden idol, and in his anger he took the two tablets with the Ten Commandments written upon them and broke them before the eyes of the people.

Moses knew that the people were doomed and that God was going to destroy them. He said He was going to do so. How did Moses change God's mind?

Deuteronomy 9:18-19 demonstrates how:

> *And I fell down before the LORD, as at the first, forty days and forty nights: I did neither eat bread, nor drink water, because of all your sins which ye sinned, in doing wickedly in the sight of the LORD, to provoke him to anger. For I was afraid of the anger and hot displeasure, wherewith the LORD was wroth against you to destroy you. But the Lord hearkened unto me at that time also* (Deuteronomy 9:18-19).

Going without food or water for forty days is fasting unto the Lord. Moses was desperate. He had been on the mountaintop with God, saw and felt His majesty, power, and glory. He knew that God kept His word. So he did what he knew touched the heart of God. He humbled himself before God in prayer and fasting. God heard Moses' cry, saw his humbleness, and changed what He said He was going to do, all because of the prayer and fasting of Moses.

Moses continued to tell them in verse 23 how angry God was at their unbelieving attitude at Kadesh-barnea when He had told them to go and possess the land. Deuteronomy 9:25 relates what Moses did at that time: "Thus I fell down before the LORD forty days and forty nights, as I fell down at the first; because the LORD had said he would destroy you."

Moses pleaded with God to change His mind.

> *I prayed therefore unto the LORD, and said, O Lord GOD, destroy not thy people and thine inheritance, which thou hast redeemed through thy greatness, which thou hast brought forth out of Egypt with a mighty hand. Remember thy servants, Abraham, Isaac, and Jacob; look not unto the stubbornness of this people, nor to their wickedness, nor to their sin: lest the land whence thou broughtest us out say, Because the LORD was not able to bring them into the land which he promised them, and because he hated them, he hath brought them out to slay them in the wilderness* (Deuteronomy 9:26-28).

Deuteronomy records God's response to the prayer and fasting of Moses:

> *And I stayed in the mount, according to the first time, forty days and forty nights; and the LORD hearkened unto me at that time also, and the LORD would not destroy thee* (Deuteronomy 10:10).

Here are two different incidents but both of them give a picture of the times of prayer and fasting of Moses. Why did Moses fast forty days? Only God knows the answer to that, but Moses' prayer was not just a flippant prayer prayed in a few minutes but was a fervent prayer that took forty days to answer.

If Moses, who was the chosen leader of Israel, and had performed miracles and done great things through God's power, thought it was necessary to spend time in prayer and fasting, how can the modern church think they are above the practices of Moses?

Another example is in the story of Jonah. According to Jonah 1:2, God said that the wickedness of Nineveh had come up before Him and He wanted Jonah to cry against it, but Jonah ran from the presence and the call of the Lord. God knew right where Jonah was and sent a storm to the ship he was traveling on, until the men on the ship threw him overboard after Jonah told them he was the cause of the storm.

Jonah could not get away from God. God followed him and prepared a fish to swallow Jonah whole, so that he could repent. And repent he did! He described it in Jonah 2:7: "When my soul fainted within me I remembered the LORD: and my prayer came in unto thee, into thy holy temple."

After Jonah's descent into the bottom of the sea by way of the belly of a fish and after God caused the fish to vomit Jonah out on dry land, Jonah was finally willing to go preach what God had spoken. What was his message? It was simple, direct, and to the point. "And Jonah began to enter into the city a day's journey, and he cried, and said, Yet forty days, and Nineveh shall be overthrown" (Jonah 3:4).

Jonah gives the response of the people:

> *So the people of Nineveh believed God, and proclaimed a fast, and put on sackcloth, from the greatest of them even to the least of them* (Jonah 3:5).

Then word came to the king of Nineveh and he also joined the people in prayer and fasting and made it mandatory for everyone including the animals to do likewise.

> *For word came unto the king of Nineveh, and he arose from his throne, and he laid his robe from him, and covered him with sackcloth, and sat in ashes. And he caused it to be proclaimed and published through Nineveh by the decree of the king and his nobles, saying, Let neither man nor beast, herd nor flock, taste any thing: let them not feed, nor drink water: but let man and beast be covered with sackcloth, and cry mightily unto God: yea, let them turn every one from his evil way, and from the violence that is in their hands* (Jonah 3:6-8).

Why did the king have the people in his kingdom and also the animals do this? Jonah 3:9 tells why: "Who can tell if God will turn and repent, and turn away from his fierce anger, that we perish not?"

The result was that God changed His mind.

> *And God saw their works, that they turned from their evil way; and God repented of the evil, that he had said that he would do unto them; and he did it not* (Jonah 3:10).

There is much power in the combination of prayer [crying mightily] to God, and true humbleness before God in fasting. He cannot turn a deaf ear to the cry of the contrite, as stated in Psalm 34:18: "The LORD is nigh unto them that are of a broken heart; and saveth such as be of a contrite spirit."

> *For all those things hath mine hand made, and*

> *all those things have been, saith the LORD: but to this man will I look, even to him that is poor and of a contrite spirit, and trembleth at my word* (Isaiah 66:2).

This is what happened in Nineveh. God did what He said He would do in Isaiah 66:2. He looked at the people who one minute had been very wicked but were now crying mightily to Him, fasting unto Him, and trembling at His word. Because of this, God changed His mind, but it did not make Jonah happy. He was very displeased and asked God to kill him, because God had not done what he had preached God would do. God then had to deal with Jonah's pride and gave him an object lesson with a gourd.

MUCH POWER!

There is much power in the combination of *prayer* and *fasting*. Jesus knew this. He practiced it before beginning His earthly ministry when He went into the wilderness.

Jesus was confronted by a situation that is related in Mark:

> *And they brought him unto him: and when he saw him, straightway the spirit tare him; and he fell on the ground, and wallowed foaming* (Mark 9:20).

This is the story of the father who took his son to the disciples for them to heal, but they could not:

> *And wheresoever he taketh him, he teareth him: and he foameth, and gnasheth with his teeth, and pineth away: and I spake to thy disciples that they should cast him out; and they could not* (Mark 9:18).

"Jesus said unto him, If thou canst believe, all things

are possible to him that believeth" (Mark 9:23). The father cried, "I believe; help my unbelief!" Then Jesus turned to the boy and said,

> *Thou dumb and deaf spirit, I charge thee, come out of him, and enter no more into him. And the spirit cried, and rent him sore, and came out of him: and he was as one dead: insomuch that many said, He is dead. But Jesus took him by the hand, and lifted him up; and he arose* (Mark 9:25-27).

Later when Jesus and the disciples were alone in the house, they asked Him why they could not cast out the spirit. Mark 9:29 states:

> *And he said unto them, This kind can come forth by nothing, but by prayer and fasting.*

Prayer and fasting change things! It changed the condition of that boy. Jesus said it: "Nothing, but by prayer and fasting." Do not try to argue away this fact. Do not become modernized in your thinking and try to do it the easy, push-button way. Jesus said it, great men and women of God have experienced it, and it works!

There is a danger in this modern generation to want everything to be easy, to not want to war in the Spirit or live a disciplined life of daily prayer, or to die to the flesh by giving oneself to times of fasting and prayer combined.

Fasting is very much a part of the Old Testament and the New Testament as proven in the following examples:

- Moses fasted forty days (Exodus 34:28),
- Daniel fasted twenty-one days (Daniel 10:2-3),
- Jehoshaphat fasted (II Chronicles 20:3),

- Nehemiah fasted (Nehemiah 1:4),
- Esther fasted (Esther 4:16),
- Ezra and the children of Israel fasted (Ezra 8:21),
- Jesus fasted forty days (Matthew 4:2),
- Paul fasted (II Corinthians 11:27),
- the disciples fasted (Acts 13:2-3; 14:23),
- and Cornelius fasted (Acts 10:30).

It simply was a practice of the Jewish culture and the early church. Fasting was not deleted when Jesus came. He emphasized it as being necessary and that some things could not happen without it.

In Matthew 6:16-17 Jesus said, "When ye fast," because He expected them to fast. He did not say, "If you fast," but He acknowledged that fasting and prayer were part of the Christian's lifestyle.

In January 1972, we left St. Louis to take the pastorate in Stockton, California. In October 1971, my husband's father, while on a hunting trip, had died immediately upon impact. The brakes of the jeep he was driving failed to operate properly while he was driving downhill. His death left a big vacancy in the church and the college, and my husband had been asked to fill this.

The first thing my husband did after the few months of grieving and pouring oil in the wounds was tell the church that we were going to be a revival church. We started having prayer and fasting chains, and much prayer was made. We knocked on doors, started bus routes, taught Bible studies, and prayed and fasted until new people started coming and revival fires began to burn.

The building was jammed and we started having double sessions, and the people kept coming. We knocked out walls and then went to triple sessions on Sunday. When we could no longer handle the crowd, we knew we had to build a new church. We found a thirty-acre parcel of land north of town [farmland] and raised the money to purchase it.

In the following words, my husband, Pastor Kenneth Haney, will tell what God did for us during this time of much prayer and fasting:

> The church had great growth. We were filled to capacity, and every service people prayed through. Most of the people we did have were poor or had middle income. The new converts came from various backgrounds. Some had been in prison, some had been drug addicts, some were atheists, and others were just normal people. Their backgrounds didn't lend to wealth, but they had desire and were willing to do anything.
>
> In 1972, when we came back to Stockton after serving in St. Louis as UPCI National Youth President, the old church and college had small debts and God enabled us to pay them off, as well as purchase thirty acres for a new building. This was all debt free, plus our engineering and plans were paid for, but we had no money with which to build.
>
> I asked the church to pray and fast about our need, and then I went to a bank my father had done business with for years. When I sat and told them my dream to build a new church that seated two thousand, they laughed at me and said they were not able to risk a loan.
>
> I walked out of that bank and went to one of the older banks in the city, Union Safe Deposit Bank, the one my grandmother Sophie

Haney used for her banking needs. I walked in and asked to see the president of the bank. In a few minutes I was seated in Don Stewart's office, and I laid out the whole scenario. Of course, he was somewhat familiar with the work of the college and the church, but the Lord sent His angels before me and the president was very interested when I told him about my proposed building. He told me when we got ready to build to come back and see him.

In a few months we were finally ready. I went back to see the president and told him it was not going to be a turnkey job. We had hired Harold Langford to run the job, he had hired a few men, and several of our members were donating their time and skills. That was our game plan in 1976.

He asked me, "How much cash do you have?" Again I went through our assets: college debt free, thirty acres debt free, plans and engineering paid for, but I could tell he wanted us to have some cash. So I told him we would have $150,000 in cash. (Now, today that doesn't sound like a lot, but thirty years ago that was a large sum.)

He asked me what it was going to cost us to build, and not knowing at that time, I just threw the figure out of $600,000. He then said he would give us $400,000, but at that moment we didn't have one penny of the $150,000.

When I left the bank, I started thinking how to get the $150,000. Two weeks from that day we were planning to have a service to raise the $150,000. We chose the theme: "We've Come This Far by Faith." I began to think about the people in our congregation, how poor they were, and how few had any extra money to give nor had the ability to acquire money. The thought came to me that they could make personal loans of $2,000-$5,000. This was how we could raise the $150,000.

So the Monday morning before the service was to be, I again went to see the bank president, Don Stewart. I explained that many of our people were new converts and had lived a sinful, negative lifestyle but were now on the right track. They wanted to live right and had good jobs. I asked him if he would make them a loan so they could give, and for those who did not qualify for a loan, would he let me co-sign for them. He looked at me amazed as if I had made an unbelievable request. I guess he was thinking there may be one or two out of the group he would let me co-sign for.

The following Sunday night we had our service. When I laid it before the church and made the appeal, many humble people began to respond. A large portion of them were the new converts. Some would say, "We are willing to give if you would help us acquire the loan." Others had the means but were unwilling to make the sacrifice.

When it was all said and done I ended up co-signing for about fifteen couples (as far as I can remember all paid back their loan with the exception of one). But we had our $150,000. I ran out of money three or four different times, but God miraculously gave us favor with the bank. The total cost to build ended up being two million dollars, but that included the

Family Center, Stockton Christian School complex, the Christian Life Center complex, and all the parking and landscape. When it was all said and done, we owed less than one million. That's how God provided.

There were thousands who received the Holy Ghost in that two-thousand-seat sanctuary, and many churches were blessed by the revival effort of Christian Life Center. We had nearly 3,000 receive the Holy Ghost in the Asian revival. In one of our crusades with Billy Cole we had 380 receive the Holy Ghost in one service. In one revival that lasted six months we had over 2,000 receive the Holy Ghost. Other churches would bring busloads to this revival.

BACK TO JOY HANEY

I remember one night during this revival that everyone was talking about the glory cloud that was above the altar area. I saw it with my own eyes: it was a blue haze. One hundred people received the Holy Ghost that night.

These things just don't happen. This all came with a price tag attached to it. We had much prayer and fasting during all this time, consistent chains of prayer and fasting. There was also stress involved in trying to keep a revival atmosphere because we had to deal with carnal people just as consistently. It was a war.

When you live in the faith level you are always under attack because it is not the norm. A few ministers in other cities could not understand the faith level of CLC and sometimes would criticize and falsely accuse because of the growth and great revival. Was it worth it? A thousand times yes! There is nothing greater than winning souls to Jesus Christ our Lord!

4

Mantle of Sacrifice

BY BOBBYE WENDELL

It would be wonderful to acquire a modest wealth to pass on to the next generations, our children and grandchildren. Financial gifts from one generation to another sometimes make life much easier for those who inherit the blessings. Certainly, for those of us who knew and endured hard times, there is a desire to save our children from our difficult experiences. However, some things need to be experienced personally to learn valuable lessons of life. There are also sentimental items, heirlooms, which pass along stories of ancestry.

I have carefully kept and sheltered certain things that were handed down from my grandmother and mother: quilting frames from my grandmother, a sugar bowl bought from a peddler who drove his wagon by the old farmhouse where my grandparents lived. And the narrow hoe, the tiny lady-sized garden hoe that my grandmother worked her garden with. These are small objects with huge memories—the valentine given to me by my dad when I was in first grade and the small, yellow taffeta dress sewed for me by my mother for a first-grade event in school. There is a Bible that belonged to a great-grandfather and many other things in my collection. Treasures of memories mingle with grandchildren and great-grandchildren who say, "Tell us the story again about when you were a little girl." And so, not only things or objects are passed on, but also the experiences and happenings that create a life testimony and sometimes the passing of a mantle.

There are certain experiences that stand out over others. I remember one that was very special, for it taught me a great lesson in my walk with God. I was brand-new in the Lord and had much to learn. One of the church ladies was to come to my house for lunch and we would pray together during the visit. As I prepared the very simple lunch I started to bake cornbread but realized that I had no baking powder. I quickly resolved the matter by deciding to make Indian bread, or hot-water cornbread. Before I could change ingredients, my friend knocked on the door. When I opened it she stood with something in her hand. She said to me, "When I started to leave my house I felt impressed to bring you some baking powder." I was so excited that God could remind someone who was so close to Him to bring such a simple thing. It made a great impression on me. God even cares about small matters in our lives.

On a particular night there was a visiting missionary and we had no money for the offering. I had prayed throughout the day for God to supply our need to support His work. Church time arrived and we were getting our coats on to leave. I was a bit heavy-hearted, for we still had no offering. As I started out the door I reached my hand into my pocket and there, deep inside and folded very small, was a five-dollar note. I was so happy and could not wait for the offering to be received. God still teaches us in small things. Someone had tucked that money in my pocket at some time and God had reserved the finding of it for the missionary service. He provides for our needs, even our need to give.

After several years in the local church, we felt a need to attend Bible school in order to better prepare ourselves for missions. God had definitely called us and we were ready to prepare. Our pastor felt it was time for us, and Texas Bible College had opened the previous year. This would be our destination. We had the desire but no finances to make the change. We packed our things in cardboard boxes and stacked them in the middle of the living room and borrowed an old cattle trailer to place our things in for the move.

We had four children: two boys and two girls. Brother Wendell called all the children, knelt together in the living room floor, and started to pray for help to make the trip. As we prayed, the Lord impressed me to read from the Bible. I read of Abraham as God directed him to leave his country in God's will. We wept and rejoiced and started packing. Soon a knock came to the door and someone stood there saying, "I want to help." He gave us twenty dollars. Immediately after he left another person came and brought one hundred dollars. This was enough to get us to Houston and to pay half of a month's rent. God provided jobs, and both of us found ourselves enrolling in Texas Bible College. It was a wonderful experience. I hope Bible school means as much to all who attend as it meant to us. In October of 1966, we were appointed as missionaries to Ethiopia, while yet students. The timing was extremely important and divinely accomplished by God's hand. He is perfect. We then had the process of deputation to fulfill.

Our deputation would become a two-year ordeal of

awaiting visas for entrance into Ethiopia. It would be a difficult project, especially for Pentecostals. Inside Ethiopia there was a great spiritual awakening, and many young people were receiving the Holy Ghost. There was not any revelation of Jesus' name prior to our arrival that we ever actually found out. We met no one who had been baptized correctly. The Ethiopian Orthodox Church, or State church, moved quickly to stop this awakening. There was a great persecution that followed.

During the two years of waiting we again faced a great trial. Brother Wendell was in an auto accident, and I was told he would probably not recover. If he did recover he would likely not ever walk without help. I found a place of prayer in the hospital. As I poured out our need again, God was faithful to answer. Great visitation of God's help and presence surrounded us, and our call was confirmed again by Brother Wendell's walking out of the hospital aided by crutches but only for a while. We were back on our way to Ethiopia.

In November 1968, Brother Wendell left for Ethiopia. His visa came through before mine and the children's. It was difficult to see him go, but there was much to do before the children and I would leave in January of 1969. Brother Wendell wrote almost every day, and we at home anxiously awaited our permission to enter Ethiopia. We shared our last Christmas in the U.S.A. for a while with family and friends and prepared our things for departure. We left Houston and were seen off by Texas Bible College President, Brother Fred Foster, and other TBC personnel and students. My parents were so broken, for they expected us to be gone from four to six years and that is a long time to be away from grandchildren.

During the weeks he was in Ethiopia before our coming, Brother Wendell stayed at the YMCA. During this stay he met many students of a technical college who frequented the YMCA for several programs offered. Those students took part in numerous projects that were approved by the school to help the poor and needy of Ethiopia. One of these projects was an area where victims of Hansen's disease, leprosy, lived. Leprosy causes the nerves to die. Body extremities, such as hands, feet, and nose simply disappear or wither away.

It would be impossible to fully describe the living conditions of those who were the "untouchables." The lepers crowded together in submission to their rejection by society. They functioned in their declared boundaries as normally as possible. They were born, lived, married, gave birth, and died just as humanity does. They created for themselves a culture and society of their own acceptance of each other. They could not enter the grounds or building of the Orthodox State Church, for they were branded by their disease. They were physically marked by the evidence of leprosy. Some slept in holes dug into the ground, some in shacks made of cardboard and pieces of tin and wood. They truly were rejected by society, but God had a plan that would be revealed to give at least some of these people a glimpse of His love. Brother Wendell was invited to be a part of the group who would attempt to improve the living quarters of these tragic people.

The long flight took us through New York, Rome, and on to Ethiopia. I cannot describe to you the feeling of landing in a strange land among a strange people and language and yet feeling as if I had come home. The children and I landed in Ethiopia at a northern city called Asmara. We did not deplane but quickly flew on to Addis Ababa, where we were reunited with Brother Wendell. It was good to have the family back together.

The next day Brother Wendell wanted to show me

the project he had been working on. We left the children to rest and drove over to the area. I was left in the vehicle while Brother Wendell went over an embankment and out of sight. People began to gather, pushing close to the open window. They had white, gauzy shawls, part of the national dress, around them and across their faces. I noticed they had deformed hands or no fingers and sometimes no hands, only stubs at the end of their arms. I was frozen with absolute fear when the shawls were lowered; some of them had disfigured faces, no eyebrows, and the nose almost gone. I had never seen anything in my life to prepare me for this. I prayed for Brother Wendell to return, and when he did walk back over the embankment he was surrounded by several of the men. He was laughing and saying strange words I could not understand. I wondered how he could be so happy in this surrounding. I found out much later.

Brother Wendell came in the car and tried to tell me what he was doing, but I told him I wanted to go home. He stopped laughing, looked at me, and said, "We are home, Bobbye. We prayed for nine years to get here. We are home, and these people are those whom God has given us to start with. If there is a church in Ethiopia, it will start here." I feebly told him I just wanted to go where the children were, to the house. I was up all night, visiting the rooms of my children and asking God and myself, "What have I done?"

The next day, Brother Wendell insisted we all go back to the project. The children were still adjusting to the culture; they were about to find out what shock really was. We put huge plastic buckets on top of our Land Rover jeep. When they were tied down, we all loaded in and drove away. The buckets were for collecting food scraps from the back door of the Hilton Hotel. Brother

Wendell had arranged for the gift of this food that hotel residents left on their plates after finishing. This would be used to feed very hungry people.

We arrived at the assigned place. Planks were laid over sawhorses to make tables. The buckets were placed on the tables. The people began to line up. Their food containers were tin cans, dirty rags, and plastic bags—whatever they could find. They pushed against each other to be first in line to insure there would be something for them. The noise was terrible—shouting, pushing children crying, everyone making noise of some kind.

My two daughters, Angie and Jeannie, were to dip out the food with large spoons. They looked so beautiful that day, with their long hair around their faces and tears washing down from fear and pity. Not one word was spoken among us all the way back home. Even Chet, our youngest, who was only nine, said nothing. Our eldest, Mark, quietly sat sheltering his little brother. When we arrived at the house I started talking, trying to make the atmosphere lighter. I said I would make a special supper. They each said, "I do not want anything to eat; I just want to see my Mamaw and Papaw." There was no evening meal, but there were many tears that night.

Closed off from the bedrooms to prevent disturbing our children, I cried and prayed through the night. Several times I visited their beds, very gently laying my hand on each one and praying, "None of these diseases. O Lord! . . . none of these diseases!"

The Ethiopian Orthodox Church was not only a religious church but also was the State church. Its impact was represented in governmental affairs. In order to perform a religious work, the Ethiopian government required of us a project, either social or educational, in order to remain in the country. We were only allowed to preach in certain areas, as dictated by the government. To fulfill this requirement, we rented an old building on a large compound. We dug a hole in the front yard, extracted the dirt and mixed it with straw bought off the donkeys' backs as they trotted past the gate with their drivers. We made *chica* and repaired the broken walls.

This building would house our "Leper Workshop and Training Center." We hired teachers who would teach cloth weaving, basket weaving, and rug weaving during the day. The workshop would also house our chapel to be used for daily devotions for the students before classes. The site of our church services and evangelistic outreach would be our first such building other than our home.

Those victims of leprosy, who were actually beggars on the streets during the day, began to line up at the gate of the workshop chapel, asking for entrance into the program. Some of them were simply ravaged by the disease; others were not so horribly scarred. It is not known how they found out the workshop was "open," but they came, sometimes lining up down the hill to the river, waiting for an opportunity to "come in." There were 500,000 people with leprosy in Ethiopia. There was no end.

Brother Wendell had designed and made a prosthesis that strapped onto the wrist to the elbow and the palm portion of the hand. This would enable the wearer to hold a tool with which to work. However, one woman who begged for a place in the school or training center had no hands, only stubs on her two wrists. Because she did not have any palms of her hands, she could not wear the prosthesis. The front parts of her feet were gone, leaving only the heel and ankle area. She could only shuffle instead of being able to walk. In order to keep her balance, the woman stuffed the front parts of old boots with rags. Brother Wendell told her she could come to the chapel and church services but could not be in the training school. She began to weep and look about her. She begged for someone to bring her a broom. We all stood there, awestruck at her intensity. She clutched the broom between her arms and began to stab at the ground with it in a sweeping motion. She slid her feet forward in the clumsy boots, not lifting the boot for fear of it sliding off. Slide . . . slide . . . sweep . . . sweep and crying and saying, "But, sir, don't you see, I am worth something." And she was . . . as is any creation of God, even those who are lepers. And there were hundreds to thousands of these people. For this woman we made an exception. She was placed. Later in a church service she asked if she could sing. Her nose was deformed and her speech was affected. She sang, "God Is So Good to Me"—not the song written here in the U.S.A. One, I am sure, that she made up as she sang.

After ten months and no one yet baptized, I was desperate for God to mine this diamond field of humanity. We had 7:30 AM chapel services five days a week, many days of training, making a hot meal of lentil porridge and native bread for the students and workers, and even washing the feet of those who had ulcers so severely on their feet. Brother Wendell had huge pans for this. He would wash the feet of the men and put salve on them and bind them. The binding would be saturated the next day to be done over again. We learned what "minister" means.

We secured a teacher, from within the lepers, who would teach the children of the leper families. The students sat on the ground under trees, using pieces of charcoal to write on pieces of wood as their writing materials. The days were all used up. Evening was welcomed each day. The longing for harvest in this land became unbearably heavy. Something had to happen.

On the mission field it is essential to have help in your home. Some things are very primitive and require much plain labor. I needed someone to help me in my home. When Brother Wendell drove in one day with the smiling lady looking toward me from the back seat of the vehicle, I knew help had arrived. She smiled all the way in, where I was introduced to her. Her name was Tsahi, which means "sun." Her smile was that bright.

She would start in the kitchen. As she turned to enter the kitchen I saw the huge ulcer on her leg. My heart sank, and I looked at my husband. I walked out to the back room and called him and asked, "Does she have leprosy?" He looked squarely at me and said, "Yes." I was horrified. In the house, with the children! This cannot be! I told him, "You have to take her away." He said he could not; she had no place to go and would be hurt again. She had been beaten terribly by other beggars. I told him very emphatically that she had to go. He sadly looked at me and said, "You may take her . . . here are the keys . . . but will you do something for us?" I asked what it was that he wanted. He asked if I would go by Calvary on the way taking her back.

DEATH TO SELF

I was numbed. Didn't he know that I *had* been to Calvary? I had been there before, but it had been to take a soul to Calvary not to lead one away. I started to cry. I took the keys and grabbed my prayer shawl. It was a nice little pink and green shawl made by someone in the Alexandria, Louisiana, church as a gift for me on the mission field. I cannot remember the dear one who gave it to me. I used it every service in the chapel church. There were reasons I used it.

I flew out of the house but did not take the lady with

me. It was time for something to happen for me. Today would be the day.

The drive to the workshop and chapel was not very far; it consisted of a road, winding down the mountainside and through the village market. The narrow road was crowded with people who seemed to have nothing to do. Every time we drove down without incident was either a tribute to our driving skills or a miracle. This day was no exception, and I arrived safely at the workshop.

It was Saturday. We did not have a Saturday service at this time. Only the guard, Wolde Gabriel, was there. He opened the gate to the property, and I drove in. Wolde had very little of his nose left on his face. His eyes looked sad and a bit wary. He would wonder what I was doing there today. I drove past him to the front door of the building. I exited the car and went into the building. It was the same as the day before, nothing changed. The sameness was the smell.

When you have over one hundred people with various degrees of infection eating away at them . . . hands, feet, faces, and bodies . . . there is a cloying, clinging odor that permeates the area. This smell never went away. Soap, disinfectant, and cleaners just added to the strength and tenacity of the smell. A smell of dying flesh, people whose desperate claim to life was: "God made me this way to test the rich man. If he gives me a coin he escapes hell and I will have bread for the day." Do you blame them? They were told they had no soul, they could never inherit heaven, and they were never allowed into the vast compounds of the existing State church. No one with physical handicap and no illegitimate person could enter the State church grounds. Many of these people would sit outside the compound of the State church, waiting for those who participated to leave and in so doing hoped that the attendees would bless them. They sat there as beggars, waiting for alms, just as those who sat at the Gate Beautiful in Acts 3. At the end of the day, these people would lie down with the feeling of clawing hunger if they were not given alms. They felt they really were the grass of the field. My heart's desire is to write more about these poor people.

I went deeper into the building. The guard, Wolde, remained at the door. His hands, or what remained of them, were held behind his back. They were covered in ulcers. I never touched them. Today was no different. I took my prayer shawl and spread it on the floor. I would kneel on it, pray, and when I went home I would throw it in the washer before using it again. I hoped it would last the length of our first term.

I started to kneel and quite firmly announced to the Lord that I had come to be "broken." With that announcement I went to my knees and started to pray. You do know that heavy smells actually can be tasted, and the smell was terrible that day.

I prayed and nothing happened. After a while, as I attempted to get through, the Lord spoke to me and said, "If you really wish to have your request (to be broken), then remove the prayer shawl." The thought of my flesh actually touching that floor was overwhelming. Some of the lepers walked barefoot daily over the floors, the smell of their infections entering the plank flooring. I could not do it. I would pray on. The voice came again, "Move the shawl." Finally, I moved the shawl. But the Lord was not finished with me yet.

As I knelt wondering if there was anything worthwhile in me, this fearful person, the Lord spoke again, "Get down." I stooped a bit; the Lord spoke and said again, "Go down" and I stooped lower. Finally, after the third time I tearfully asked the Lord, "I'm down . . . how much further?" He said, "Until there is no further down." I went down, stretched out on my face and frontal body.

I literally lay before the Lord with weeping. I would feel to turn my face and I would understand that I was to stay as I was. Something was happening. After time, later to be judged about three hours, something like a dam broke inside me. Fear of disease and strangeness and filth poured from me. From the lower regions of my body to the flowing out of sounds and words from my mouth, the Lord delivered me. I would never be the same again. There would be a harvest. There would be a church and a people.

Leprosy is a type of sin. We were in a house where lepers could enter and be ministered to. This was a victory. It was already in progress. As God prevailed in the prayer meeting that day and cast out the fear, He would prevail over the spiritual leprosy of sin. There would be fulfillment of Psalm 68:31, my call to Ethiopia. "Princes shall come out of Egypt; Ethiopia shall soon stretch out her hands unto God."

I arose, as a new person, and went out of the building. The guard simply looked at me. I said, "Wolde, give me your hands." He held them behind his back. I asked him again, and finally he extended them. I took his hands in mine and said to him, "You will never have to hide your hands from me again." And he never did.

The foundation of the enemy's resistance was broken that day, and soon we would baptize our first Ethiopians in Jesus' name. In those beginning days of harvest, there were twenty-seven leper people who were baptized in Jesus' name and several received the Holy Ghost. Many other acts of God's mercy were done, and doors began to open to fulfill Psalm 68:31.

As stated earlier, I have gathered many small gifts and treasures through the years and collected many books. These are not expensive items, but they are part of my life. I have files of letters and cards received, some from children with their innocent thoughts. There are memories of great prayer experiences, church services, messages, and hours of meaningful worship. At times the memories of it all flood my mind and soul. Time has huge and powerful wings; it travels so quickly. We must stop and question, "What do we pass to our own children and to the next generation?" Surely, the small keepsakes and treasures will be carefully divided among children and grandchildren, although there are no great sums of money to leave.

As the apostles of the early church said to the lame man who was placed at the Beautiful Gate to beg alms, even as the lepers previously described, "Silver and gold have I none; but such as I have give I thee: In the name of Jesus . . . rise up and walk" (Acts 3:6). And the man walked.

May the next generation believe and practice faith in the name and Word of the Lord, that they may see the harvest accomplished. Their inheritance of the Apostolic truth and doctrine with power is a promise that the best is yet to come.

5

Mantle of Hunger

BY JOY HANEY

True hunger makes people desperate. Joseph Rotbaum-Ribo, who arrived in Sachsenhausen at the end of 1944 and was one of the survivors of the concentration camps, shares the following incidents that occurred on the march from Sachsenhausen to another location:

> Every additional day of the march became more difficult, the rations we received were finished, more and more people fell to the ground and couldn't finish. At one point along the road there was a dead horse and many prisoners, in spite of the dangers involved, ran to the carcass and started cutting out pieces of meat. Soon the German guards, with shouts, beat the prisoners back into the column. Those few lucky ones who succeeded could be seen holding pieces of red horsemeat and chewing it while walking.
>
> Hunger was the predominant problem, and prisoners were eating the roots of shrubbery growing in the forest or cut out pieces of bark

from trees and scraped out the inside and ate.

Hunger will make people do things they would not do otherwise. It drives them to unusual acts and causes them to lose their sense of pride and decorum. When hunger dictates, reason fails to impress or influence the mind.

Jesus talked about hunger in Matthew 5:6: "Blessed are they which do hunger and thirst after righteousness: for they shall be filled." Righteousness is God and the things of God, as all man's righteousness is as filthy rags as stated in Isaiah 64:6: "But we are all as an unclean thing, and all our righteousnesses are as filthy rags."

It pleases God for someone to seek and hunger after Him. He said "blessed" are they who do so. This was spoken to Mary when she was chosen to be the mother of Jesus. The angel said to her, "Thou . . . art highly favoured, the Lord is with thee: blessed art thou among women."

To be blessed of God is the highest attainment on earth. He said this would be for those who hunger and thirst after Him.

David had this hunger for God and described it in Psalm 42:1: "As the hart panteth after the water brooks, so panteth my soul after thee, O God." It was not a casual thirst, but one of a running deer, perhaps one that was hunted and his throat was parched. He needed water to survive.

So it is with those who hunger after God. Jesus said, "If any man thirst, let him come unto me, and drink" (John 7:37). Jesus was referring to the prophecy concerning the Holy Spirit, and as He is the source of the initial pouring out of His Spirit, He is also the source for those who hunger for more of Him.

David penned the yearning of his soul in Psalm 63:1, which says it well: "O God, thou art my God; early will I seek thee: my soul thirsteth for thee, my flesh longeth for thee in a dry and thirsty land, where no water is."

Psalm 63:2 tells what he was yearning for: "To see thy power and thy glory."

When you have a thirst, yearning, or passion to see God's power and His glory, to experience true revival, or to witness the supernatural, God said that it would come to those who hunger for it.

HUNGER FOR THE THINGS OF THE SPIRIT

If you want God to use you, then you must hunger after Him as stated in the following paragraph:

> Nearness to God is essential if we are to be used of God. He chooses the vessel nearest His hand. This has always been true. The apostles, martyrs, missionaries, and saints who have finished their work and have gone on before, as well as those who live today, prove the statement that we must be in closest relationship with Christ if we are to be entrusted with the gift of power. It is when we are in the secret place of the Most High that we learn God's will concerning us.
>
> —J. WILBUR CHAPMAN[3]

Elisha hungered for this. He saw the supernatural at work in the life of Elijah and he wanted that. Every time Elijah would tell him that he was going to another city, Elisha would say, "As the LORD liveth, and as thy soul liveth, I will not leave thee" (II Kings 2:2). He clung to that which he desired. He was not going to let it get out of his sight. Tenaciously, he stayed on the heels of Elijah, watching his every move, noting his response to things.

His heart beat more quickly when he would see a miracle, and desire came up in his throat to have that ministry. He wanted it more than life.

They went from Gilgal to Bethel. When they arrived there, Elijah told Elisha to stay [tarry] there.

Then he said he was going from Bethel to Jericho and again he said: "Stay [tarry] here."

The third time, as Elijah was going from Jericho to Jordan, he again said, "Stay [tarry] here."

Three times Elisha said, "As the LORD liveth, and as thy soul liveth, I will not leave thee" (II Kings 2:6). Elisha wanted what Elijah had. He desired to work miracles and operate in the supernatural.

Finally, after Elijah smote the Jordan River with his mantle and the two walked on dry ground to the other side, Elijah said unto Elisha, "Ask what I shall do for thee, before I be taken away from thee. And Elisha said, I pray thee, let a double portion of thy spirit be upon me" (II Kings 2:9).

If Elisha had not clung to Elijah and stayed with him each step of the way, he probably would not have gotten what he desired.

Another man who desired a birthright that was not rightfully his received it because he hungered for it. It is interesting to note that Jacob was at Bethel also. This is where his covenant was validated by God.

As he slept, he dreamed of a ladder that was set up on earth and the top reached to heaven, and the angels were descending and ascending on it. The Lord God stood above it and talked with him and told him, "And, behold, I am with thee, and will keep thee in all places whither thou goest, and will bring thee again into this land; for I will not leave thee, until I have done that which I have spoken to thee of" (Genesis 28:15).

Later when he was coming face to face with his brother Esau, from whom he had stolen the birthright, in his fear he went alone to pray to God. During this time he wrestled with an angel and said, "I will not let thee go, except thou bless me" (Genesis 32:26). Jacob had that tenacity that would not let go of the promise, and he got it.

This same intense desire for the things of the Spirit must become ours. We should passionately seek to have the Holy Spirit burning within us as a flame of fire. The following poem says it well:

DIVINE ENERGY

Give me the love that leads the way,
The faith that nothing can dismay,
The hope no disappointments tire,
The passion that will burn like fire.
Let me not sink to be a clod:
Make me Thy fuel, Flame of God.

—Unknown Author[4]

As a young minister's wife I always loved the things of God, but as I grew a little older, there welled up within me such hunger for more than just the norm. I would read of the revivals in Ireland, Wales, England, and then the Azusa outpouring, and I would fall before the Lord on my knees and cry out for this same fervor and power. This thirst for more of God flamed within me and was in my mind continually. I could be talking to people and going through normal duties, but all the while I was dominated by this urgent longing and passion.

I remember my first forty-day fast. I had such a hunger for God and the things of the Spirit that it drove me to much prayer and fasting. There were times on the fast when I felt like the Spirit was carrying me, and at other times it was more difficult to fast. It doesn't matter whether the Spirit carries you or it is pure death to the flesh, fasting must be embarked upon to live in the atmosphere of the early church and have great revivals and miracles abounding among us.

I also remember as a young minister's wife, after hearing stirring messages by anointed preachers that I would pray desperately, weeping profusely, crying: "God use me for your glory! Take my *nothing* and make it *something*. Take my little lunch, break it, and bless it to feed the multitude." Little did I realize what I was praying! The breaking was the painful part, the blessing the reward, but I learned that *the bleeders are the blessers*. You have to bleed to bless, for God uses broken things. He does not allow you to be broken just to be broken, but it is for a greater purpose. When you are hurt or stabbed in the heart, it is He that is allowing the breaking, so that He can use you to bless the multitudes.

Jesus' body was broken so a world could be saved; not only was His body broken, but also His heart. He came unto His own, but they received Him not. He was rejected, spit upon, and despised by the religious leaders. Paul relates the words of Jesus in I Corinthians 11:24: "And when he had given thanks, he brake it, and said, Take, eat: this is my body, which is broken for you: this do in remembrance of me."

Jesus talked about this *death to self* or the breaking in John 12:24-26: "Except a corn of wheat fall into the ground and die, it abideth alone: but if it die, it bringeth forth much fruit. He that loveth his life shall lose it; and he that hateth his life in this world shall keep it unto life eternal. If any man serve me, let him follow me."

Theologians say that Jesus was referring to His own death when He spoke about the corn of wheat dying.

Yes, Jesus knew He would die physically, but even so, He also threw out the challenge to all His followers that they would have to die also. Not so much physical death, but death to self, made alive unto God as stated in Romans 6:11: "Likewise reckon ye also yourselves to be dead indeed unto sin, but alive unto God through Jesus Christ our Lord."

This type of serving the Lord, giving all unto Him begins with hunger for him!

HUNGER FOR REVIVAL—REACHING THE LOST

All great revivals start with prayer and hunger for God. Mr. J. C. Lamphier, a lay missionary in New York City, was greatly burdened for the souls of that city. Almost daily in the lecture room of the Old Dutch Church he would go alone to pray for a genuine revival. He announced a weekly prayer meeting to be held at the noon hour on Thursday. On September 23, 1857, the doors were open for the first of these meetings. It started small, but before long the numbers increased and it became a daily prayer meeting. This meeting room overflowed, so other places were secured and prayer meetings were held all over New York City. These were known as the Fulton Street prayer meetings, where many people humbled themselves and cried out to God for revival.

Not long after these prayer meetings were established, one of the men who attended them moved to Philadelphia. There he sought to start a prayer meeting also. At first he was jeered at, but God looked with favor upon him and the little group. It wasn't long until the meeting room was too small, and they secured a bigger building, until finally they ended up renting a building that seated over four thousand people.

Soon this noonday prayer meeting spread from coast to coast. W. T. Stead, one of the editors of the *British Review of Reviews*, made a statement about "The Revival of 1857" in America. He said, "It was the direct precursor of the great civil war and the emancipation of the slaves."[5]

The work of God is done when people surrender themselves unto Him and His will and place their lives in His hands, as the following paragraph describes:

> The chisel cannot carve a noble statue—it is only cold, dead steel. Yet neither can the artist carve the statue without the chisel. When, however, the two are brought together, when the chisel lays itself in the hands of the sculptor, ready to be used by him, the beautiful work begins. We cannot do Christ's work—our hands are too clumsy for anything so delicate, so sacred; but when we put ourselves into the hands of Christ, his wisdom, his skill, and his gentleness flow through us, and the work is done.
>
> – Phillips Brooks[6]

This happened at Azusa over one hundred years ago. A man, William Seymour, who hungered after God and started prayer meetings, became a vessel that affected people around the world. What happened there still has an influence on this generation.

HUNGER FOR THE WORD

Psalm 119:131 expresses this hunger: "I opened my mouth, and panted: for I longed for thy commandments."

I have felt this emotion many times—eagerly looking forward to reading and studying the Bible. The Word has enlightened, thrilled, lifted, challenged, convicted, soothed, and healed me. It has given me answers and shown me the way when there was no way.

I would rather read the Bible than any other book on earth, and I enjoy studying and researching subjects. It is so invigorating and stimulating! There is nothing on earth that has greater power than the Word of God.

Once when I spoke at a ladies' retreat, after service they served some refreshments. Across the table from me sat a lady named Laurinda Salvador, who lived on the Palau Island until her adult life. She shared with me the following story:

> I was eight years old when I was adopted by my uncle, my mother's brother. My stepmother wasn't a very good mother. She was hateful and unloving. I loved to be in the trees sitting, watching birds flying and chirping, wishing I was a bird flying to escape this unloving and uncaring stepmother.
>
> One day my friend at school told me a story of Jesus she had heard at Sunday school. I began to ask her to tell me more about this loving Jesus. We began to spend our recess time alone and away from everybody, where she could tell me more about Jesus. I began to fall in love with this Jesus she was telling me about. I couldn't wait until recess time. We had picked out a spot just up the hill behind the schoolhouse. That was our special place.
>
> I asked my stepmother one Sunday morning if I could go to Sunday school. She told me, "No! Do not ask me again. That's just wasting your time. You have a lot of work to do."

Not long after this, I developed a boil on my left knee. It became worse so that I could not walk, only crawl. I was left alone to look after myself and care for my boil. I was eleven years old and didn't know anything of how to take care of it, so I cried myself to sleep at night because of the pain. I dared not cry in front of my stepmother.

There was an old man from another village whom my parents brought home to work for them. He was a Christian man and appeared to be very compassionate. It wasn't very long until he found out what kind of a stepmother I had, so he would sneak me a Bible so I could read it while he was working.

One day my stepmother was gone for a whole day. The old man brought me his Bible to read while he went down the hill to do the gardening. It was 3:00 in the afternoon when I was reading the Bible intensively, trying to read as much as I could before my stepmother came home. My left leg was flexed because I could not stretch or stand on it. It was swollen and very painful.

I was reading the eighth chapter of the book of Matthew when I felt movement in my leg. I closed the Bible and watched my leg moving and suddenly my leg stretched out, the boil on my knee started going down. I watched the swelling going down, and the boil disappeared. I got scared and began to look around me. Not a single soul was around, just the birds flying. I stood, putting weight on my left leg, feeling no pain. I picked up the Bible, looked at it almost afraid of the power of the Book I was reading.

I took the Bible and ran to where the old man was working. I shouted, "I got healed. This book has power!" We both jumped up and down and rejoiced, thanking God for His power in the Word. I will cherish His Word until the end of time.

What a compelling story! This lady's attitude and reverence toward the Word are an indictment toward some Christians who rarely pick up the Bible except to go to church. Oh, the power they are missing!

We should love His Word and delight in its pages as expressed in the following verses:

Psalm 119:47: "And I will delight myself in thy commandments, which I have loved."

Psalm 119:97: "O how love I thy law! it is my meditation all the day."

Psalm 119:140: "Thy word is very pure: therefore thy servant loveth it."

Psalm 119:167: "My soul hath kept thy testimonies; and I love them exceedingly."

If a person could only have one thing and had to choose between a Bible and one million dollars, and chose the money, he or she would be foolish because the Bible is worth more than gold as declared in Psalm 119:127: "Therefore I love thy commandments above gold; yea, above fine gold."

The Word is sweet and brings good things into the life of the one who reads it, as stated in Psalm 119:103: "How sweet are thy words unto my taste! yea, sweeter than honey to my mouth!"

It brings success as spoken of in Joshua:

> *This book of the law shall not depart out of thy mouth; but thou shalt meditate therein day and night, that thou mayest observe to do according to all that is written therein: for then thou shalt make thy way prosperous, and then thou shalt have good success* (Joshua 1:8).

It is important for minister's wives to develop a hunger for the Word, for it is the very foundation of Christianity, doctrine, and truth. Without it they are powerless, ineffective in spiritual warfare, and overcome by life. The Word is life! In it you will find God, as the following paragraph reveals:

> The great reservoir of the power that belongeth unto God is His own Word—the Bible. If we wish to make it ours, we must go to that book. Yet people abound in the church who are praying for power and neglecting the Bible. Men are longing to have power for fruit bearing in their own lives and yet forget that Jesus has said: 'The seed is the Word of God.'
>
> —R. A. TORREY[7]

THE THRILL OF HIS WORD

I thrill with the ecstasy of His Word!
It seeps into my spirit and I am stirred;
To the depths of my being comes new love
That can only be found from inspiration above.

Ink written on pages by God's revelation
Brings true life and blood-bought salvation.

Integrity and righteousness are found in its pages;
Forever it will be throughout all the ages.

A wonderful Volume of truth and power;
It is very much needed for this fateful hour.
The answers are there for anyone to find;
They need only to look—commit them to mind.

Oh how precious, His promises divine,
And to think that each one is all mine!
When the winds blow, and long is the night,
I just reach for the glorious Book of light.

Greater words were never spoken by men;
Anointed, they bring deliverance from sin.
It's a hammer, a fire, light, and a sword.
The subject throughout is Jesus the Lord.

—JOY HANEY

SUMMARY

Hungering after the things of the Spirit is crucial to walking in the realm of the supernatural. It cannot be business as usual; neither can it be boring ritual. Whatever it takes to regain hunger—that is, if you have known it but now do not possess it—then that is what needs to be done. Get it back at any cost! If you have never known hunger, then seek God in prayer and fasting, asking Him to put a hunger inside you for the things of the Spirit.

Oh, the yearning of the soul for the things of God! What utterances too wonderful to talk about when sitting in His presence! What glories to behold as His Spirit is at work among those who crave for His glory to be manifested! The absolute longing to be in the presence of His majesty is indescribable. Nothing compares to the sheer joy that comes when this hunger is filled. As Jesus said, "Blessed are they which do hunger and thirst after righteousness [or after Him]!"

6

Mantle of Truth

BY JOY HANEY

❖ ❖ ❖

What is truth? This was asked by Pilate after Jesus had spoken these words: "Thou sayest that I am a king. To this end was I born, and for this cause came I into the world, that I should bear witness unto the truth. Every one that is of the truth heareth my voice" (John 18:37).

Jesus said in John 14:6: "I am the way, the truth, and the life: no man cometh unto the Father, but by me." So truth is Jesus! He said that He came into the world to bear witness of the truth, and every one that is of the truth listens to His voice. I want to hear everything I can about truth, which is Jesus Christ! The two main truths that we need to pass from generation to generation is the truth of baptism in Jesus' name and the Oneness message: Jesus is God!

TRUTH OF THE ONENESS MESSAGE: JESUS IS GOD!

I woke up this morning with the thought singing over and over in my brain: "Jesus is God!" It was so strong; I knew that God wanted me to write this part of the book today. This is a truth that must be taught to our children and to all those who will listen. The whole Bible is about Jesus, as the following paragraph demonstrates:

> The central theme of the Bible is Jesus Christ. It begins with Jesus Christ as the bud in Genesis that produces the flower, the finished fruit in Revelation, the coming, ruling King of kings. The Old Testament conceals Christ, the New Testament reveals Christ. The Old Testament veils Christ, the New Testament unveils Christ. The Old Testament is Christ concealed, the New Testament is Christ revealed. The Old Testament contains Christ, the New Testament explains Christ. It is, indeed, 'The Jesus Book.'
>
> —JOHN R. BISAGNO[8]

Isaiah gives the prophecy that a Son would be born, but it conceals the *name* of the Son but tells who He is:

> *For unto us a child is born, unto us a son is given: and the government shall be upon his shoulder: and his name shall be called Wonderful, Counseller, The mighty God, The everlasting Father, the Prince of Peace* (Isaiah 9:6).

Who was the Son who was prophesied to be born?

Wonderful!
Counselor!
The mighty God!
The everlasting Father!
The Prince of Peace!

The time came for the prophecy to be fulfilled. It was time for the Son to be born. That is when the angel Gabriel was sent from God to a virgin named Mary. She was engaged to be married to a man named Joseph. Luke describes Mary's encounter with the angel:

> *And the angel came in unto her, and said, Hail, thou that art highly favoured, the Lord is with thee: blessed art thou among women. And when she saw him, she was troubled at his saying, and cast in her mind what manner of salutation this should be. And the angel said unto her, Fear not, Mary: for thou hast found favour with God* (Luke 1:28-30).

Through the ages, men had wondered what name God would call Himself when He would manifest Himself in the flesh. For the first time in the history of mankind, the angel was about to unveil the sacred name to a young virgin. Luke 1:31 reveals the name: "And, behold, thou shalt conceive in thy womb, and bring forth a son, and shalt call his name JESUS."

How Mary must have trembled just to think that she was the first person to know this name. Her soul was enraptured, and her heart must have been pounding with gratitude and excitement as the angel continued to speak to her about the miracle birth of Jesus:

> *He shall be great, and shall be called the Son of the Highest: and the Lord God shall give unto him the throne of his father David: and he shall reign over the house of Jacob for ever; and of his kingdom there shall be no end* (Luke 1:32-33).

Mary was concerned because she knew she could not have a child without having intimate relations with a man, and she voiced this in Luke 1:34: "Then said Mary unto the angel, How shall this be, seeing I know not a man?"

The miracle of the birth was about to be revealed.

> *And the angel answered and said unto her, The Holy Ghost shall come upon thee, and the power of the Highest shall overshadow thee: therefore also that holy thing which shall be born of thee shall be called the Son of God* (Luke 1:35).

Luke gives the fulfillment of the first part of the angel's prophecy:

> *And she brought forth her firstborn son, and wrapped him in swaddling clothes, and laid him in a manger; because there was no room for them in the inn* (Luke 2:7).

There may not have been a welcoming committee on earth, but there was one in the heavenlies.

> *And there were in the same country shepherds abiding in the field, keeping watch over their flock by night. And, lo, the angel of the Lord came upon them, and the glory of the Lord shone round about them: and they were sore afraid. And the angel said unto them, Fear not: for, behold, I bring you good tidings of great joy, which shall be to all people. For unto you is born this day in the city of David a Saviour, which is Christ the Lord. And this shall be a sign unto you; Ye shall find the babe wrapped in*

swaddling clothes, lying in a manger. And suddenly there was with the angel a multitude of the heavenly host praising God, and saying, Glory to God in the highest, and on earth peace, good will toward men (Luke 2:8-14).

Isaiah 9:6 had been fulfilled: the Son was born! He was the mighty God, the everlasting Father, and the Prince of Peace. John recorded also that Jesus was God:

In the beginning was the Word, and the Word was with God, and the Word was God. . . . And the Word was made flesh, and dwelt among us [Jesus], (and we beheld his glory, the glory as of the only begotten of the Father,) full of grace and truth (John 1:1, 14).

There was an incident where a group of Jews told Jesus that He had a devil, and they asked Him if He was greater than their father Abraham. Jesus answered them in John:

Yet ye have not known him; but I know him: and if I should say, I know him not, I shall be a liar like unto you: but I know him, and keep his saying. Your father Abraham rejoiced to see my day: and he saw it, and was glad (John 8:55-56).

This enraged them, and their answer is recorded in John 8:57: "Then said the Jews unto him, Thou art not yet fifty years old, and hast thou seen Abraham?"

Jesus triumphantly told them who He was in John 8:58: "Jesus said unto them, Verily, verily, I say unto you, Before Abraham was, I am."

Jesus was saying, "I am the mighty God, which was prophesied by the prophet Isaiah." This same phrase was used when Moses asked God whom he should say sent him:

> *And Moses said unto God, Behold, when I come unto the children of Israel, and shall say unto them, The God of your fathers hath sent me unto you; and they shall say to me, What is his name? what shall I say unto them? And God said unto Moses, I AM THAT I AM: and he said, Thus shalt thou say unto the children of Israel, I AM hath sent me unto you* (Exodus 3:13-14).

Several thousand years later Jesus was saying to the Jews who were questioning Him: Before Abraham was, I AM! This was the same I AM!

Jesus said several times, I AM, as shown in the following examples:

John 6:35: "And Jesus said unto them, I AM the bread of life: he that cometh to me shall never hunger; and he that believeth on me shall never thirst." John 6:33, 51 explains this bread: "For the bread of God is he which cometh down from heaven, and giveth life unto the world. . . . I am the living bread which came down from heaven: if any man eat of this bread, he shall live for ever: and the bread that I will give is my flesh, which I will give for the life of the world."

John 8:12: "Then spake Jesus again unto them, saying, I AM the light of the world: he that followeth me shall not walk in darkness, but shall have the light of life." When Jesus spoke that He was the light of the world, some of the Pharisees did not believe Him. John 8:19 records their question and His answer: "Then said they unto him, Where is thy Father? Jesus answered, Ye neither know me, nor my Father: if ye had known me, ye should have known my Father also." Isaiah had prophesied that the Son would be called the everlasting Father. Jesus was telling them that if they knew Him, they would know the Father. John 10:30 substantiates this when Jesus said, "I and my Father are one."

John 10:9-10: "I AM the door: by me if any man enter in, he shall be saved, and shall go in and out, and find pasture. The thief cometh not, but for to steal, and to kill, and to destroy: I AM come that they might have life, and that they might have it more abundantly."

John 10:11: "I AM the good shepherd: the good shepherd giveth his life for the sheep."

John 11:25: "Jesus said unto her, I AM the resurrection, and the life: he that believeth in me, though he were dead, yet shall he live."

After Jesus had been crucified and buried in a sealed tomb, three days later He arose from the dead. He truly was the resurrection and the life, but there were some who did not believe and one of them was a disciple named Thomas.

> *Except I shall see in his hands the print of the nails, and put my finger into the print of the nails, and thrust my hand into his side, I will not believe* (John 20:25).

Eight days later, the disciples were sitting in a closed room, and Jesus appeared in their midst, although the door was shut.

> *Then saith he to Thomas, Reach hither thy finger, and behold my hands; and reach hither thy hand, and thrust it into my side: and be not faithless, but believing. And Thomas answered and said unto him, My Lord and my God* (John 20:27-28).

One theologian said that Thomas was a Jew, had studied the law, and knew that there was only *one* God, and this was not just a slip of words but was revealed to him who Jesus really was: his Lord and God! All Jews had learned from a child and quoted this truth daily, "Hear, O Israel: The LORD our God is one LORD" (Deuteronomy 6:4).

Another rabbi of rabbis was Saul, who was intent on persecuting the church because he did not believe the doctrine the disciples were preaching daily in the temple, that Jesus was God. This enraged Saul. As he was on his way to Damascus to persecute the Christians, suddenly a light shined round about him, and he fell to the earth and heard a voice saying, "Saul, Saul, why persecutest thou me?"

> *And he said, Who art thou, Lord? And the Lord said, I am Jesus whom thou persecutest: it is hard for thee to kick against the pricks. And he trembling and astonished said, Lord, what wilt thou have me to do? And the Lord said unto him, Arise, and go into the city, and it shall be told thee what thou must do* (Acts 9:5-6).

Notice that Saul was astonished at this revelation, that the Lord was Jesus. He was a Jew, and all Jews know that there is only one Lord.

While Saul and the men who were with him journeyed to Damascus, the Lord was giving Ananias a vision and telling him to go meet Saul to give him the gospel. Ananias talked back to God and told Him that he had heard of the evil Saul was doing to the saints. But the Lord told him to go and meet him, that He had chosen Saul to bear His name before the Gentiles, kings, and the children of Israel.

> *And Ananias went his way, and entered into the house; and putting his hands on him said, Brother Saul, the Lord, even Jesus, that appeared unto thee in the way as thou camest, hath sent me, that thou mightest receive thy sight, and be filled with the Holy Ghost* (Acts 9:17).

Notice Ananias said, THE LORD, EVEN JESUS. This was one Jew speaking to another, and they were both schooled in the law and understood fully the impact of their words. They were saying as Thomas said, "Jesus, my Lord and my God."

God gave Saul a new name: Paul. He became a powerful influence in helping to establish the early church and wrote many letters to the different churches. Paul understood that Jesus was God.

> *And without controversy great is the mystery of godliness: God was manifest in the flesh, justified in the Spirit, seen of angels, preached unto the Gentiles, believed on in the world, received up into glory* (I Timothy 3:16).

God was manifest in the flesh: that was Jesus! God was justified in the Spirit: that was Jesus! God preached unto the Gentiles: that was Jesus! God was believed on in the world: that was Jesus! And God was received up into glory: that was Jesus! Jesus is God.

There is only *one* God, and there will only be *one* sitting on the throne. The devils know this as is stated in James 2:19: "Thou believest that there is one God; thou doest well the devils also believe, and tremble."

Revelation 4:2 shows that there is only one who sits on the throne: "And immediately I was in the spirit: and, behold, a throne was set in heaven, and one sat on the throne." Jesus Himself spoke in Revelation:

> *I am Alpha and Omega, the beginning and the ending, saith the Lord, which is, and which was, and which is to come, the Almighty. . . . Fear not; I am the first and the last: I am he that liveth, and was dead [Jesus]; and, behold, I am alive for evermore, Amen; and have the keys of hell and of death* (Revelation 1:8, 17-18).

Revelation 22:1-3 talks about the pure river of water proceeding "out of the throne of God and of the Lamb [one throne]." Revelation 22:4 states that God and the Lamb are one and the same: "And they shall see his face [his face-singular]; and his name [his name-singular] shall be in their foreheads." One name, one face, that of Jesus Christ!

TRUTH OF WATER BAPTISM IN JESUS' NAME

This truth was not manufactured by some organization, but it is contained in the Holy Bible and spoken by men who were trained under the ministry of Jesus. They spoke what He had taught them. When the Holy Ghost was poured out on the Day of Pentecost and those receiving the Spirit began to speak in other tongues, it was an amazing thing. There were those who heard this and asked, "What meaneth this?" Others said they were full of new wine, which means they were drunk, but Peter stood and began to preach to them that "This is that which was spoken by the prophet Joel" (Acts 2:16).

Peter continued to preach to them, and when he had finished they were pricked in their hearts and asked, "Men and brethren, what shall we do?" His answer to them is still the way to be saved and is for all generations, as Acts proves:

> *Then Peter said unto them, Repent, and be baptized every one of you in the name of Jesus Christ for the remission of sins, and ye shall receive the gift of the Holy Ghost. For the promise is unto you, and to your children, and to all that are afar off, even as many as the Lord our God shall call* (Acts 2:38-39).

The church went forth in the power of the name of *Jesus* from that time onward. Acts 3:16 demonstrates that they emphasized the name of Jesus as shown in the story of the lame man being healed: "And his name [*Jesus*] through faith in his name [*Jesus*] hath made this man strong."

This angered the priests and the Sadducees, and they put the apostles in prison. Then they brought them before the Sanhedrin, where the high priests and others were gathered, and asked them by what *name* they had done this (referring to the healing of the lame man).

Peter again was the spokesman and stood and told them how they had crucified Jesus, and clinched it with Acts 4:12: "Neither is there salvation in any other: for there is none other name under heaven given among men, whereby we must be saved."

The rulers of the Sanhedrin let them go but commanded them not to teach or preach in the name of Jesus, but they did just that and were placed in prison the second time. This time the angel of the Lord came and opened the prison doors and told them to speak in the Temple all the words of this life. So they did, and again the leaders put them in shackles and brought them before the rulers, telling them they were filling Jerusalem with their doctrine. It was the intent of the Sanhedrin to kill them, but Gamaliel told them to leave it be: "But if it be of God, ye cannot overthrow it; lest haply ye be found even to fight against God" (Acts 5:39).

So instead of killing them, they beat them and commanded that they should not speak in the name of Jesus. What did they do? Acts 5:42 states: "And daily in the temple, and in every house, they ceased not to teach and preach Jesus Christ."

Everyone in the early church was baptized in the name of Jesus. It was not until later, in AD 325 under Constantine, that they begin to baptize in the titles instead of the name. Jesus said to baptize in the name of the Father [Jesus] (John 5:43), name of the Son [Jesus] (Matthew 1:21), name of the Holy Ghost [Jesus] (John 14:26).

When Philip went to the city of Samaria and preached Jesus to them, they were filled with the Holy Ghost and baptized in the name of Jesus. Acts 8:16: "(For as yet he was fallen upon none of them: only they were baptized in the name of the Lord Jesus.)"

Notice the phrase: *he was fallen upon none of them. He* is the Holy Ghost. Jesus is *He*. Jesus said in John:

> *Even the Spirit of truth; whom the world cannot receive, because it seeth him not, neither knoweth*

> *him: but ye know him; for he dwelleth with you, and shall be in you* (John 14:17).

Jesus was saying, "I am with you, but I shall be in you."

Jesus had just spoken earlier in John 14:6: "I am the way, the truth, and the life: no man cometh unto the Father, but by me."

How marvelous that Jesus is truth and Jesus is the Holy Ghost as shown in John:

> *But the Comforter, which is the Holy Ghost, whom the Father will send in my name, he shall teach you all things, and bring all things to your remembrance, whatsoever I have said unto you* (John 14:26).

When the apostles heard that Samaria had received the word of God, they sent Peter and John to join Philip. "Then laid they their hands on them, and they received the Holy Ghost" (Acts 8:17). While revival was happening in Samaria, the angel of the Lord spoke to Philip and told him to go down to Gaza, and he went. There he found a man of Ethiopia, a eunuch of great authority under Candace, queen of the Ethiopians. He had come to Jerusalem to worship and was returning and sitting in his chariot reading Isaiah. "Then the Spirit said unto Philip, Go near, and join thyself to this chariot" (Acts 8:29). So Philip went to the eunuch and asked him if he understood what he was reading. And he said, "How can I, except some man should guide me?" Philip began to explain what the phrase in Isaiah meant. "Then Philip opened his mouth, and began at the same scripture, and preached unto him Jesus" (Acts 8:35).

When they came to some water, the eunuch said,

"Here is water; what doth hinder me to be baptized?" Acts 8:38 records what happened: "And he commanded the chariot to stand still: and they went down both into the water, both Philip and the eunuch; and he baptized him." Philip had baptized all the converts in Samaria in the name of Jesus, as was stated in Acts 8:16, and was sent by the Spirit to do the same for the eunuch in the desert. He did not change the formula for baptism on his way there. It was still in the name of Jesus. It was not a sprinkling, but it was by immersion in the water.

Colossians substantiates this:

> *Buried with him in baptism, wherein also ye are risen with him through the faith of the operation of God, who hath raised him from the dead* (Colossians 2:12).

You do not bury people by sprinkling dirt on them; they are put down, into the earth, just as a new believer is put down, into the water, signifying death to self and the old man and coming up a new man in Christ Jesus.

When Peter preached to the house of Cornelius, he preached the same message of baptism as shown in Acts 10:48: "And he commanded them to be baptized in the name of the Lord."

Paul also commanded his converts to be baptized in the name of Jesus. When he came to Ephesus, he found certain disciples and asked them,

> *Have ye received the Holy Ghost since ye believed? And they said unto him, We have not so much as heard whether there be any Holy Ghost. And he said unto them, Unto what then were ye baptized? And they said, Unto John's baptism* (Acts 19:2-3).

Paul then explained to them that John baptized with the baptism of repentance but that he had preached unto them "that they should believe on him which should come after him, that is, on Christ Jesus" (Acts 19:4).

Acts records what happened:

> *When they heard this, they were baptized in the name of the Lord Jesus. And when Paul had laid his hands upon them, the Holy Ghost came on them; and they spake with tongues, and prophesied* (Acts 19:5-6).

Ephesians 4:5-6 sums up that there is only *one* way to baptize and that there is only *one* Lord: "One Lord, one faith, one baptism, one God and Father of all, who is above all, and through all, and in you all."

The world will pass away, but truth will live forever as expressed in the following poem:

TRUTH NEVER DIES

Truth never dies. The ages come and go;
The mountains wear away; the seas retire;
Destruction lays earth's mighty cities low;
And empires, states, and dynasties expire;
But caught and handed onward by the wise,
Truth never dies.

Though unreceived and scoffed at through the years;
Though made the butt of ridicule and jest;
Though held aloft for mockery and jeers,
Denied by those of transient power possessed,
Insulted by the insolence of lies,
Truth never dies.

—AUTHOR UNKNOWN[9]

7

Mantle of Holiness

BY JOY HANEY

When I was growing up as a child, we used to sing the following song that is not sung much any more, but it still should be the cry of our heart:

> To be like Jesus,
> To be like Jesus,
> On earth I long to be like Him;
> All through life's journey
> From earth to glory
> I only ask to be like Him.

This is what holiness is: it is having the character of Christ and His purity live inside of us and dominate what we do inwardly and outwardly. We advertise what we are by what we do and what we wear. It tells the world around us *whom* we belong to and by *whose* standards we live.

We are His to dwell in as stated in Ephesians 2:21-22: "In whom all the building fitly framed together groweth unto an holy temple in the Lord: in whom ye also are builded together for an habitation of God through the Spirit."

What a wonder! We are the habitation of God! God walks in us, lives in us, and sits on the throne of our hearts. We are His as stated in I Corinthians 6:19-20: "What? know ye not that your body is the temple of the Holy Ghost which is in you, which ye have of God, and ye are not your own? For ye are bought with a price: therefore glorify God in your body, and in your spirit, which are God's."

Our body and spirit belong to God. He has bought us with His blood (Acts 20:28). "According as he hath chosen us in him before the foundation of the world, that we should be holy and without blame before him in love" (Ephesians 1:4).

He wants us to be holy and bring Him glory.

> *That we should be to the praise of his glory, who first trusted in Christ. In whom ye also trusted, after that ye heard the word of truth, the gospel of your salvation: in whom also after that ye believed, ye were sealed with that holy Spirit of promise, which is the earnest of our inheritance until the redemption of the purchased possession, unto the praise of his glory* (Ephesians 1:12-14).

We are bought! He bought us! He wants us to glorify Him, to be His praise and glory:

> *But ye are a chosen generation, a royal priesthood, an holy nation, a peculiar people; that ye should shew forth the praises of him who hath called you out of darkness into his marvellous light* (I Peter 2:9).

Glorify, glorify, and glorify Him some more! That is what we are supposed to do, glorify Him in our bodies and spirit. Holiness is living in such a way that we bring glory to our God, the one who purchased us.

God, sin, and uncleanness do not mix. If God is in us, then that means there is no room for anything that would besmirch His name and Spirit!

> *And what agreement hath the temple of God with idols? for ye are the temple of the living God; as God hath said, I will dwell in them, and walk in them; and I will be their God, and they shall be my people. Wherefore come out from among them, and be ye separate, saith the Lord, and touch not the unclean thing; and I will receive you* (II Corinthians 6:16-17).

He dwells in us! We are temples of the Lord! We are His habitation! What an awesome privilege that He would want to take up residence inside of us, that He would even desire to walk in us and shine through us! We must protect that privilege!

God wants us to separate ourselves from whatever is contrary to His mind and ways. We must be separate from the world in desires, motives, and acts. Hebrews 7:26 describes Christ: "For such an high priest became us, who is holy, harmless, undefiled, separate from sinners, and made higher than the heavens."

Just as Jesus was holy, undefiled, and separate from sinners, we are to be also. Although He ministered to sinners, He did not accept their ways or mingle His ideas with theirs but walked according to the Word of God and righteousness.

He came to earth to seek and to save those who were lost. He came with miracle power, forgiveness, and great light. He said He was the Light of the world, the Door, the Way, the Truth, and the Life.

If Christ is the Way, we are the signboards.
If Christ is the Truth, we are the examples.
If Christ is the Life, we are the messengers.
If Christ is the Door, we are the doorkeepers,
to open it to others.
If Christ is the Vine, we are the fruit
bearing branches.[10]

We are signboards to show others the way, examples of His power and forgiveness, messengers of His love, and are bringing others to Jesus Christ, showing forth the fruit of the Spirit. We act as His ambassadors as stated in II Corinthians 5:20: "Now then we are ambassadors for Christ."

Glorify, glorify, and glorify Him even more! That is what we are to do! How do we glorify Him? Everything we *are*, everything we *do*, everything we *say*, and everything we *love* must reflect His glory.

I John plainly says that the will of God is to love not the world:

> *Love not the world, neither the things that are in the world. If any man love the world, the love of the Father is not in him. For all that is in the world, the lust of the flesh, and the lust of the eyes, and the pride of life, is not of the Father, but is of the world. And the world passeth away, and the lust thereof: but he that doeth the will of God abideth for ever* (I John 2:15-17).

The question is this: "Do I talk like the world, do I act like the world, or do I look like the world?" If I do, I need to change something because I'm not a light, I'm blending with them, mingling—I'm not separate. There is not a distinction.

A Christian and the world simply cannot be on the same page in their thinking. They do not mix! There must be a difference, letting everyone know whose side you are on as the following story depicts:

> During one of the Italian wars, some recruiting officers came to a small town. Men and boys of all ages were recruited and joined in a parade, armed with swords, guns, and sticks. An old lady was so stirred by the spectacle that she shouldered her broom and fell in line. Proudly she marched along, keeping perfect step with the others. Onlookers jeered at the old lady. They asked, "What good can you do in a battle?" She replied, "Not much, but I want everybody to know whose side I am on!"
>
> -REVEREND WILLIAM MCCARRELL, D.D.

This is how a Christian should be. Let everyone know whose side you are on: God's or the world system. The oil of the Holy Ghost is inside us, and we should never try to mix it with the weak, watered-down substance of worldly things; it is impossible for them to mix. The true purity of Christ is always to be separated from that which is tainted and suggestive.

> *Abstain from all appearance of evil. And the very God of peace sanctify you wholly; and I pray God your whole spirit and soul and body be preserved blameless unto the coming of our Lord Jesus Christ* (I Thessalonians 5:22-23).

There should not be a balancing act between good and evil, but a complete separation. The *spirit, soul,* and *body* are to be blameless—the *whole* person.

The *spirit* is the part of man which "knows"—his mind, as shown in I Corinthians 2:11: "For what man knoweth the things of a man, save the spirit of man which is in him? even so the things of God knoweth no man, but the Spirit of God."

The *soul* is the seat of the affections, desires, emotions, and the active will, the self. An example of this is the prayer of Christ in Matthew 26:38: "My soul is exceeding sorrowful."

God wants our spirit, our mind, our soul, emotions, desires, and affections, our whole self and whole body to be holy. It is impossible for one part to be holy and another part to be unholy. Mankind cannot separate itself into compartments; it is impossible to do so.

Holiness is a heart matter. It begins with our spiritual heart. Our talk, the way we dress and act are outward manifestations of the heart. They tell others if the holiness of God's presence lives inside us. Our behavior, mannerisms, and dress (our whole image) should reflect His glory.

After David's sin, his need for holiness was why he prayed so desperately,

> *Create in me a clean heart, O God; and renew a right spirit within me. Cast me not away from thy presence; and take not thy holy spirit from me* (Psalm 51:10-11).

David knew that in order to have God's Holy Spirit, he needed God to create in him a new heart, to give him a renewed spirit, and to show him mercy.

We must be made new in Christ as stated in II Corinthians 5:17: "Therefore if any man be in Christ, he is a new creature: old things are passed away; behold, all things are become new."

This is emphasized by Ephesians 4:24: "And that ye put on the new man, which after God is created in righteousness and true holiness."

Only God can create in us a new heart that is filled with righteousness and true holiness. That is why the Word of God is so essential to the continuation of God's holiness. It shapes our thoughts, regulates our emotions, and counsels us on how to behave as a Christian. It shines a glaring light on sin and saves us from falling into pitfalls that lead to anguish and despair.

Titus 2:12 instructs how to live: "Teaching us that, denying ungodliness and worldly lusts, we should live soberly, righteously, and godly, in this present world."

There it is in a nutshell: live *soberly* (give serious thought to these matters), *righteously* (virtuously and blameless), and *godly* (holy, without sin).

John Wesley's mother taught her children the following rule about sin:

> Would you judge the lawfulness of a pleasure? Take this rule: Whatever weakens your reason, impairs the tenderness of your conscience, obscures your vision of God, or takes away the relish of spiritual things or increases the authority of your body over your mind, *that is sin*.

Sin separates us from God, because a holy God does not mix with unholy sin. It is that simple. You do not have to be a chemist to understand this principle. It is worldliness or godliness. There is no in-between. The two just do not mix.

The world has a system, but God has a higher order of requirements for His children. The world in its wisdom is darkness compared with the true Light of the World.

Ephesians 5:11 states: "And have no fellowship with the unfruitful works of darkness."

The world has a spirit that is different than God's Spirit as expressed in I Corinthians 2:12: "Now we have received, not the spirit of the world, but the spirit which is of God."

> The *world* is a spirit, and is expressed in things. It defies exact definition because it is a spirit. The closest working definition I have found is that of John Wesley: "Whatever cools my affection toward Christ is in the world."
>
> —Dr. V. Raymond Edman[11]

Colossians 3:1-2 speaks about those affections: "If ye then be risen with Christ, seek those things which are above. . . . Set your affection on things above, not on things on the earth."

May the holiness of Christ permeate our whole being, and may we shine with His glory as we are in the world but not of the world as Philippians states:

> *That ye may be blameless and harmless, the sons of God, without rebuke, in the midst of a crooked and perverse nation, among whom ye shine as lights in the world* (Philippians 2:15).

We must be made conformable unto Christ: "That I may know him, and the power of his resurrection, and the fellowship of his sufferings, being made conformable unto his death" (Philippians 3:10) and not be conformed to the world standards as stated in Romans:

> *And be not conformed to this world: but be ye transformed by the renewing of your mind, that ye*

may prove what is that good, and acceptable, and perfect, will of God (Romans 12:2).

When the subject of holiness is talked about, immediately standards of dress are thought of as holiness. Holiness is within, and involves our speech, thoughts, right actions toward people, godly attitudes, our morals, our measure of love for God and others, and everything that we do. Holiness involves the whole person.

Even though God's holiness involves so much more, the mantle of outward holiness is important, just as the condition of our heart is, and it must be passed down from generation to generation as stated in II Thessalonians 2:15: "Stand fast, and hold the traditions which ye have been taught, whether by word, or our epistle." It acts as a statement to the world that we are different and we dress according to the Scriptures that command us to be modest and not by the standards of the world.

In like manner also, that women adorn themselves in modest apparel, with shamefacedness and sobriety. . . . But (which becometh women professing godliness) (I Timothy 2:9).

The image that a Pentecostal woman portrays: her dress, her long, uncut hair, her modesty, and all that goes with making her project godliness—this needs to be preserved. If you have questions on this subject, I advise you to get books written by Pentecostal authors and read them, and study the Bible until it becomes clear to you why these things are important.

The thing to remember is that all that we are, all that we do, all that we look like, all that we say, it all should reflect the fact that we are temples of God, and we should bring Him glory by the choices we make.

> *Know ye not that ye are the temple of God, and that the Spirit of God dwelleth in you? If any man defile the temple of God, him shall God destroy; for the temple of God is holy, which temple ye are* (I Corinthians 3:16-17).

I AM A TEMPLE

I am a Temple, made white and pure;
By God's own blood came the cure.
From sin He washed me and made me whole,
Created me holy: in heart, mind, and soul.

I am a Temple, a special dwelling place
Where others can see His glory in my face;
A habitation for His majesty divine,
What a wonder and privilege that are mine!

I am a Temple, not by what I've done,
But Jesus the victory at Calvary won!
So all who desire to be called His own
Can boldly come and approach His throne.

I am a Temple fashioned by God's hand;
Let me ever for righteousness stand.
May I guard daily the glory in me!
And obey and follow His Word explicitly.

I am a Temple by the Master's design.
Let me reflect the glory that's not mine,
Walk humbly remembering that self has died;
In this temple, let Him be glorified!

—Joy Haney

Mantle of Faith

BY JOY HANEY

God has given every lady a beautiful mind. He made it and He wants it to be filled with faith and belief in Him. He has great things planned for His church, but they must believe to attain them. Ephesians gives a glimpse into His plan:

> *That the God of our Lord Jesus Christ, the Father of glory, may give unto you the spirit of wisdom and revelation in the knowledge of him: the eyes of your understanding being enlightened; that ye may know what is the hope of his calling, and what the riches of the glory of his inheritance in the saints, and what is the exceeding greatness of his power to usward who* believe, *according to the working of his mighty power* (Ephesians 1:17-19).

The power of belief is demonstrated in the story told about the people who planned to build the Tower of Babel, which would reach into the heavens. God did not like this, because they were doing it not unto Him but to themselves. His response to their effort is recorded in Genesis:

> *And the* L*ORD said, Behold the people is one, and they have all one language; and this they begin to do: and now nothing will be restrained from them, which they have imagined to do* (Genesis 11:6).

God recognized that nothing could stop what they had believed or imagined to do. There is power in what a person believes.

Belief is strong as steel. It is a certainty, a conviction, or confidence that something will happen. Belief knows before it is done. We all have beliefs, and they are like pictures in our mind.

Ezekiel 8:12 talks about the imaginations or the chambers of imagery in the mind: "Then said he unto me, Son of man, hast thou seen what the ancients of the house of Israel do in the dark, every man in the chambers of his imagery?" Every woman has a chamber of imagery. There are pictures on the walls of those chambers, pictures of health or pictures of disease, pictures of failure or pictures of success, pictures of doubt or pictures of faith.

Some of those pictures need to stay in the chamber of our imagery, but some need to come down. Paul addressed this in II Corinthians:

> *Casting down imaginations, and every high thing that exalted itself against the knowledge of God, and bringing into captivity every thought to the obedience of Christ* (II Corinthians 10:5).

We all need to examine the pictures we are allowing to hang in the corridors of our mind. It is a private place;

no one is allowed there but God, of course. He wants us to believe in His Word, to pray His Word, to stand on His Word, and to press on and believe in Him even when we feel like fainting.

David wrote in Psalm 27:13, "I had fainted, unless I had believed." David, who was destined to be king, did not become king for twenty years. His faith was tested. The present king, Saul, had him hunted like a vagabond. David roamed the hills with men who were, according to I Samuel 22:2, in distress, in debt, and who were discontented. No wonder David had to see something that was beyond him, to remember a promise from the prophet; in order to keep from fainting, he had to believe something that was not yet.

It was Hebrews 11:1 in a nutshell: "Now faith is the substance of things hoped for, the evidence of things not seen." David grabbed hold of the evidence that could not be seen with the human eye but could be seen in the chambers of his imagery. He remembered the words of the prophet who pronounced that he would be king, and in his mind he saw the oil that had been poured over his head when Samuel anointed him.

This same "evidence" faith happened in the New Testament with the woman who had a disease known as an issue of blood. She got a picture of her healing *before* she was healed. Matthew 9:21 records, "For she said within herself, If I may but touch his garment, I shall be whole." She believed before it was done. This was the evidence in her mind.

The result of that evidence was when Jesus said, "Daughter, be of good comfort; thy faith hath made thee whole" (Matthew 9:22). What you *believe* affects your faith. Her faith in Jesus healed her.

We need to speak our belief; speak out loud the faith

that is inside us. Speak to the elements. Jesus said to do this in Mark:

> *And Jesus answering saith unto them, Have faith in God. For verily I say unto you, That whosoever shall say unto this mountain, Be thou removed, and be thou cast into the sea; and shall not doubt in his heart, but shall believe that those things which he saith shall come to pass; he shall have whatsoever he saith* (Mark 11:22-23).

II Corinthians 4:13 says it also: "We having the same spirit of faith, according as it is written, I believed, and therefore have I spoken; we also believe, and therefore speak."

Belief or faith is a spirit that permeates your mind and makes you speak it. This happened in the story of Caleb and Joshua. Caleb stilled the people and said in Numbers 13:30: "Let us go up at once, and possess it; for we are well able to overcome it."

The men who went up with him believed differently. They said in Numbers 13:31: "We be not able to go up against the people; for they are stronger than we."

God called their report an evil report as stated in Numbers 13:32: "And they brought up an evil report."

God became angry that the people followed the report of the ten instead of the two who said, "We are well able!" God's response, after listening even further to the grumbling and complaining of the disbelieving people, is found in Numbers:

> *And the LORD said unto Moses, How long will this people provoke me? and how long will it be ere they believe me, for all the signs which I have shewed among them?* (Numbers 14:11).

Numbers tells what God had in store for those who did not believe:

> *Say unto them, As truly as I live, saith the LORD, as ye have spoken in mine ears, so will I do to you: your carcases shall fall in this wilderness; and all that were numbered of you, according to your whole number, from twenty years old and upward, which have murmured against me* (Number 14:28-29).

God had a different reward for Caleb as stated in Numbers:

> *But my servant Caleb, because he had another spirit with him, and hath followed me fully, him will I bring into the land whereinto he went; and his seed shall possess it* (Numbers 14:24).

Joshua and Caleb had the spirit of faith, and the ten had the spirit of fear. The two said, "We can!" and the ten said, "We can't because the people are stronger than us and we are as grasshoppers in our own sight." They looked at themselves for their power; they did not look to God. God does not give fear as stated in II Timothy 1:7: "For God hath not given us the spirit of fear; but of power, and of love, and of a sound mind."

God said Caleb had *another spirit*: that was the spirit of faith; whereas the ten had the spirit of fear. Which spirit will you allow to rule you?

II Kings 2:9 talks about the spirit of faith that Elijah had, and Elisha wanted it: "And Elisha said, I pray thee, let a double portion of thy spirit be upon me." When the sons of the prophets saw Elisha part the waters with the mantle they said, "The spirit of Elijah doth rest on

Elisha" (II Kings 2:15). Elisha *saw* those waters part *before* they parted. He believed!

Jesus pronounced a blessing on those who believe before they see. Thomas would not believe until he had felt and touched the nail prints in Jesus' hands, and then he believed. John 20:29 states: "Jesus saith unto him, Thomas, because thou hast seen me, thou hast believed: blessed are they that have not seen, and yet have believed."

Augustine said, "Faith is to believe what we do not see, and the reward of this faith is to see what we believe."[12]

The story of Florence Chadwick is relevant to this subject. She was the first woman to swim the English Channel in both directions, and at age thirty-four, her goal was to be the first woman to swim from Catalina Island to the California coast.

The Fourth of July morning in 1952, when she embarked on her journey, was foggy and cold. Swimming in frigid waters with sharks cruising near her, only to be driven away by rifle shots fired by someone in the support boats, Florence was given encouragement by her mother and trainer, who were in the boat nearest her. While millions watched her on national television, she asked to be pulled out with only a half-mile to go.

Later, while thawing her chilled body, she told a reporter, "Look, I'm not excusing myself, but if I could have *seen* land I might have made it." Neither fatigue nor the cold water caused her defeat; it was the fog. She gave up because she was unable to see the land.

The good news is that two months later, she tried it again, but this time she made it. She knew that somewhere behind that fog was land, and she kept her goal clearly pictured in her mind, letting nothing deter her.

She became the first woman to swim the Catalina Channel, eclipsing the men's record by two hours!

To believe is to see something happen before it transpires. As Jesus stated, "Blessed are they that have not seen, and yet have believed." Faith does not have to see something tangible in order to believe. It believes; then the miracle occurs.

With God all things are possible! The problem is not with God, but it is with us. We must believe that He is able to do exceedingly, abundantly, and above all we ask or think! He can do all things!

I received an email recently from a lady who was asking me if there were some things that God could not do. She had gone on a fast and her faith was high, and she believed things that others did not. When she spoke her faith, there were those who doubted whether God could and would do some things.

When I read this, the following two verses of Scripture in Jeremiah immediately came to my mind.

Jeremiah 32:27: "Behold, I am the LORD, the God of all flesh: is there any thing too hard for me?" That question is answered in *Jeremiah 32:17*: "Ah Lord GOD! behold, thou hast made the heaven and the earth by thy great power and stretched out arm, and there is nothing too hard for thee."

God is God, and besides Him there is no other power.

> *But without faith it is impossible to please him: for he that cometh to God must believe that he is, and that he is a rewarder of them that diligently seek him* (Hebrews 11:6).

Daniel believed in his God; therefore, his rewarding God kept him in the time of trouble. This great power—the unlimited power of God, the "with God all things are possible" power was at work in Daniel's life.

It was belief in God that protected Daniel from the lions in the lions' den as stated in Daniel 6:23: "So Daniel was taken up out of the den, and no manner of hurt was found upon him, because he *believed* in his God."

There is power in what you believe.

Andrew C. Ivy, M.D. states:

> Religious attitudes of mind help keep men's bodies healthy. Attitudes such as love, faith, hope, unselfishness, forgiveness, tolerance, and a desire for justice and truth set the body at rest and strengthen it physically.
>
> Anti-religious attitudes such as hate, envy, jealousy, guilt, vanity, malice, vindictiveness, and selfishness put a strain on the body and are conducive to the development of disease.[13]

Why not choose to believe that God has all power to heal not just anyone, but you personally? Faith can make you whole as shown in the following instances:

In the story told in Matthew 8:5-13, a centurion asked Jesus to heal his servant, who was grievously tormented, sick of palsy. Jesus told him He would come and would heal him.

The centurion answered Jesus and said, "Lord, I am not worthy for you to come under my roof. Just speak a word. I'm a man under authority and have soldiers under me. I say, 'Go,' and my men go. 'Come,' and they come."

Matthew 8:10 states: "When Jesus heard it, he marvelled, and said to them that followed, Verily I say unto you, I have not found so great faith, no, not in Israel."

Notice the clincher in Matthew:

> *"And Jesus said unto the centurion, Go thy way; and as thou hast believed, so be it done unto thee. And his servant was healed in the selfsame hour"* (Matthew 8:13)

Jesus said, "As thou hast believed!"

When two blind men followed Jesus, crying, "Thou Son of David, have mercy on us," Jesus turned to them and said: "Believe ye that I am able to do this?" (Matthew 9:28). After they said, "Yes," Jesus touched their eyes and said, "According to your faith be it unto you" (Matthew 9:29).

Jairus, a ruler of the synagogue, went to Jesus and told Him that his daughter was at the point of death, and asked Jesus to come to lay hands on her and heal her. Jesus started to go with him, and while on the way, He was stopped by the woman with the issue of blood. When she touched Him in faith, Jesus asked, "Who touched my clothes?" Then the woman fell down and told Jesus everything. "And he said unto her, Daughter, thy faith hath made thee whole; go in peace, and be whole of thy plague" (Mark 5:34).

While this was happening, a servant came and told Jairus that his daughter had died. Jesus heard his words and immediately said, "Be not afraid, only believe" (Mark 5:36). Jesus knew that fear cancels faith; that is why He said, "Be not afraid, *only believe*!"

Jesus loved to meet people who had faith and often upbraided those who did not. This was the case in the story of the lake experience. Jesus and the disciples got into a boat and were going to the other side of the lake when there arose a great storm of wind, and the waves beat into the ship so that it was full of water. Jesus was sound asleep in the back of the boat, and when the disciples found Him, they said, "Master, carest thou not that we perish?"

> *And he arose, and rebuked the wind, and said unto the sea, Peace, be still. And the wind ceased, and there was a great calm. And he said unto them, Why are ye so fearful? how is it that ye have no faith?* (Mark 4:39-40).

Then the disciples feared exceedingly and said one to another, "What manner of man is this, that even the wind and the sea obey him?" They went from *fear* to *wow*! He created the lake and the wind. He was in charge even though it looked like He was not. We need to continually keep in our minds about Him that wow! He has all power in heaven and in earth and can do all things exceedingly, abundantly, above what we ask or think.

It is a sin not to believe as stated in Psalm 78:17: "And they sinned yet more against him by provoking the most High in the wilderness."

The psalmist tells of all God did for the children of Israel, how they questioned Him, and His response in the following verses:

Verse 19: "Can God furnish a table in the wilderness?"

Verse 20: "Can he give bread also? can he provide flesh for his people?"

Verse 21: "Therefore the LORD heard this, and was wroth." WHY?

Verse 22: "*Because they believed not in God,* and trusted not in his salvation."

Then in verses 23-29 the psalmist described all the miracles God did for them. In Psalm 78:32 he summarized the scenario of their unbelief and of God's wonders: "For all this they sinned still, and believed not for his wondrous works."

This same spirit of unbelief was present in the New Testament in a certain group of people. Mark 6:5-6 says: "And he could there do no mighty work, save that he laid his hands upon a few sick folk, and healed them. And he marvelled because of their unbelief."

May the spirit of faith grab hold of us as never before and the spirit of doubt and unbelief be cast aside! No matter what is going on in your life, just believe. No matter if your family is going through great trial, only believe.

Dr. Raymond Edman wrote:

> Faith is dead to doubts, dumb to discouragements, blind to impossibilities, knows nothing but success. Faith lifts its hands up through the threatening clouds, lays hold of Him who has all power in heaven and on earth. Faith makes the uplook good, the outlook bright, the future glorious. Believe your beliefs that are founded on the Word of God, and doubt your doubts that come from disease, despair, disappointment, or disobedience. Doubt paralyzes—faith vitalizes.[14]

Doubt paralyzes—faith vitalizes! This happened to Jehoshaphat when he was surrounded by the enemy. He was afraid (II Chronicles 20:3), and he did not know what to do. So first he proclaimed a fast and then he prayed. II Chronicles 20:12 records his prayer: "O our God, wilt thou not judge them? for we have no might against this great company that cometh against us; neither know we what to do: but our eyes are upon thee."

God heard their prayer and spoke to them as stated in II Chronicles:

> *Thus saith the LORD unto you, Be not afraid nor dismayed by reason of this great multitude; for the battle is not yours, but God's. To morrow go ye down against them: . . . Ye shall not need to fight in this battle: set yourselves, stand ye still, and see the salvation of the LORD with you, O Judah and Jerusalem: fear not, nor be dismayed; to morrow go out against them: for the LORD will be with you* (II Chronicles 20:15-17).

After they received this word from God, they fell to the ground and worshiped Him.

The next morning Jehoshaphat organized singers to go forth in the battle singing. He told them in II Chronicles 20:20: "Believe in the LORD your God, so shall ye be established." Then the singers went forth singing, "Praise the LORD; for His mercy endureth for ever!"

II Chronicles records the victory:

> *And when they began to sing and to praise, the LORD set ambushments against the children of Ammon, Moab, and mount Seir, which were come against Judah; and they were smitten. . . . And when Judah came toward the watch tower in the wilderness, they looked unto the multitude, and, behold, they were dead bodies fallen to the earth, and none escaped* (II Chronicles 20:22, 24).

When we believe in God He always brings a victory!

Spurgeon wrote,

> Faith links me with Divinity. Faith clothes me with the power of Jehovah. Faith insures every attribute of God in my defense. It helps me to defy the hosts of hell. It makes me march triumphant over the necks of my enemies.[15]

One preacher said: "I suppose that if all the times I have prayed for faith were put together, it would amount to months. I used to say, 'What we want is faith; if we only have faith we can turn our city upside down, or rather right side up.' I thought that some day faith would come down and strike me like lightning. But faith did not seem to come. One day I read in the tenth chapter of Romans, 'Faith cometh by hearing, and hearing by the word of God.' I had closed my Bible and prayed for faith. I now opened my Bible and began to study, and faith has been growing ever since."

Faith comes by the Word of God and by praying in the Holy Ghost as stated in the following verses of Scripture:

Romans 10:17: "So then faith cometh by hearing, and hearing by the word of God."

Jude 20: "But ye, beloved, building up yourselves on your most holy faith, praying in the Holy Ghost."

This is the best way I know to grab hold of the mantle of faith: by devouring the Word of God, by committing it to mind, and by praying in the Holy Ghost and then practicing faith, living in the Spirit and not in the flesh.

We did this in our ladies' prayer group. We prayed in the Holy Ghost and expounded the anointed Word until the level of faith was so high that God was able to do exceeding and abundantly above what we were asking Him to do, astonishing some with His glory and power!

This spirit of faith has caused many miracles to be. I've seen God do so many wonderful and miraculous things by simply operating in the Spirit according to His will and Word.

One of those miracles occurred in 1991, when my husband and I were asked to speak at the European conference, which was held in Holland. The first night after he spoke, several ladies came up to me and asked me to pray for them. One lady in particular asked me to pray that she could have a baby. She had wanted one for years, and no matter what she did, she remained childless. The doctors couldn't help her; only God could heal and open her womb.

I laid hands on her and began to pray for her, and after the prayer, I said, "You shall hold a baby in your arms. God will give you your desire." She had a worried look on her face, and I said to her, "Smile! You need to relax, for God is going to do a miracle in your life." She began to rejoice and all the ladies with her began to praise the Lord.

About a year and a half later I received a letter from France, and as I opened it, a photograph of a little boy fell out. Because it was written in French, I had one of the girls who was attending Christian Life College translate it for me. She told me that it was from a lady I had prophesied over and she wanted me to see her miracle. The Lord had opened her womb and she now had a baby. When I shared this with the ladies of our prayer group there was much rejoicing over this miracle.

What makes this miracle so fresh in my mind is that this year [2006], when my husband flew to France to speak at their General Conference, the story was told to him all over again by Missionary Nowacki. The lady just happened to be his sister [I did not know this when I prayed for her], but my husband met the mother, father, and the fourteen-year-old son and had his picture taken with him. They all talk about his being a miracle. He is a very handsome young man. His mother and father are ministers who pastor one of the churches in France—wonderful people of God.

What happened was that I spoke a word of faith under the anointing of the Holy Ghost, the lady received the word in faith, and God did the rest.

These things just do not happen. There must be a desire for this kind of faith. When people are hungry enough to pray and fast until they enter into the dimension where the Spirit operates, it will happen. "According to your faith, be it unto you!" Faith comes by hearing the Word of God, by praying in the Holy Ghost, and by exercising that faith.

9
Mantle of Faithfulness

BY JOY HANEY AND NILAH MEAN

❖❖❖

JOY HANEY

God does not give to everyone the same abilities. There are those with one talent, some with three, and others with five. Some gained the advantage in natural ability, heritage, in training, or through opportunities. Even though people do not have the same talents, God did give to everyone the ability to be faithful. He requires of a steward that he [or she] be found faithful over that with which they are entrusted. Although God rewards the person who is found faithful, in none of His teachings is there found leniency for those who are not faithful.

Faithfulness is giving what you have to the Master and then sticking with the job that He asks you to do, being faithful where He places you, and doing whatever He needs you to do. Paul spoke about this surrender of self in Romans:

> *I beseech you therefore, brethren, by the mercies of God, that ye present your bodies a living sacrifice,*

> *holy, acceptable unto God, which is your reasonable service* (Romans 12:1).

Where the place is that you find yourself, be assured that there will be hardship. Life is not easy and often things get worse before they get better, but no matter what, just keep being faithful. The hard things are the learning times.

> There are few positions in life in which difficulties have not to be encountered. These difficulties are, however, our best instructors, as our mistakes often form our best experience. We learn wisdom from failure more than from success. We often discover what will do by finding out what will not do. Great thoughts, discoveries, inventions have very generally been nurtured in hardship, often pondered over in sorrow and established with difficulty.
>
> —PAXTON HOOD[16]

The apostle Paul's life was filled with great difficulty, but he did not let those things keep him from doing the will of God. His success was in his surrender. He wrote in Galatians:

> *I am crucified with Christ: nevertheless I live; yet not I, but Christ liveth in me: and the life which I now live in the flesh I live by the faith of the Son of God, who loved me, and gave himself for me* (Galatians 2:20).

Paul was saying that his will, his desires, and his ways were crucified to the higher will of Jesus Christ.

There were others who worked with Paul who had the same spirit of surrender and faithfulness. Philippians 2:25 introduces one of them: "Yet I supposed it necessary to send to you Epaphroditus, my brother, and companion in labour, and fellowsoldier, but your messenger, and he that ministered to my wants."

Epaphroditus' attitude toward the work of God is described in Philippians 2:30: "Because for the work of Christ he was nigh unto death, not regarding his life, to supply your lack of service toward me."

He did not regard his own life but kept giving even when it hurt. This is commitment. Being faithful is being committed. On a humorous note, a hen and a hog were passing a church, and they heard the pastor's sermon on "How can we help the poor?" The hen said, "I know what we can do. We can give them a ham and egg breakfast." The hog protested, saying, "The breakfast would be only a contribution for you, but for me it would mean total commitment."

Being faithful means we give our life not just as a contribution once in a while, but we give it totally surrendered to Jesus Christ and His will.

Hebrews 12:2 says, "Looking unto Jesus the author and finisher of our faith; who for the joy that was set before him endured the cross, despising the shame." Jesus made a commitment, not a contribution. He was committed to the cross. Whatever we give ourselves to the most, to that we are most committed.

Jesus was committed to winning the lost. John 4:4 states: "And he [Jesus] must needs go through Samaria." He did not just go to get a drink; it was a call of the Spirit. May our lives be such—led by the Spirit, doing the will of God. Jesus talked to the woman whom many people would ignore and told her about the water that would spring up into everlasting life. She then went and told her friends, "Come, see a man, which told me all things that ever I did: is not this the Christ?" (John 4:29).

The result of His commitment: "And many of the Samaritans of that city believed on him for the saying of the woman, which testified, He told me all that ever I did" (John 4:39).

The church is being sent to every nationality and country with the gospel of Jesus Christ. The command is given in Luke 14:21: "Go out quickly into the streets and lanes of the city, and bring in hither the poor, and the maimed, and the halt, and the blind."

The command is continued in Luke 14:23: "Go out into the highways and hedges, and compel them to come in, that my house may be filled."

Jesus desires that all people would hear the gospel and that His house would be filled with hungry people. It is up to each of us to help make that happen, even when it looks difficult or impossible as stated in the following paragraph.

> Faith is taking God at His word. It does not require a big army as in the case of Gideon, or the ability to see ahead as when Abraham went out into a new land, but it does require a change in direction as in Paul's life—also a clean life as in Joseph's life. Faith involves belief but is more than belief. It is an unseen spiritual principle which enables us to cooperate with God so things can be accomplished that could not without Him. With God directing, great things can happen.
>
> —Sue Rogers Mitchell[17]

It is the keeping on when things are tough that gets the job done. "A diamond is a piece of coal that stuck to the job."

I Corinthians promises a reward:

> *Therefore, my beloved brethren, be ye stedfast, unmoveable, always abounding in the work of the Lord, forasmuch as ye know that your labour is not in vain in the Lord* (I Corinthians 15:58).

The call is going forth today. The call is old, but the message remains fresh and new. Jesus told His followers in Mark 16:15: "Go ye into all the world, and preach the gospel to every creature." Verse 20 says, "And they went."

May God give you the courage to go forward, each of you doing what you can do for Jesus Christ, and together we can make a difference. We will be faithful no matter what! Life is not easy, things get tough, but leaders must have the tenacity and bravery to push onward in spite of circumstances as described in the following paragraph:

> No man can accomplish that which benefits the ages and not suffer. Discoverers do not reap the fruit of what they discover. Reformers are pelted and beaten. Men who think in advance of their time are persecuted. They who lead the flock must fight the wolf.
>
> —HENRY WARD BEECHER[18]

Someone once said, "If you want a place in the sun, you have to expect some blisters." The ministry is not all sun and roses; there are also blisters and thorns. To be successful in what you do takes work, endurance, and faith even when there are painful thorns and even daggers that pierce your heart.

During the hurtful times, discouragement can set in and cause you to want to give up the fight. You must keep on and not get tired of the journey, but let yourself be refreshed in the Lord as you encounter these times that would threaten to kill you. Paul needed this refreshing as stated in Romans 15:32: "That I may come unto you with joy by the will of God, and may with you be refreshed."

Sometimes God sends people your way who refresh you as demonstrated in I Corinthians:

> *I am glad of the coming of Stephanas and Fortunatus and Achaicus: for that which was lacking on your part they have supplied. For they have refreshed my spirit and yours: therefore acknowledge ye them that are such* (I Corinthians 16:17-18).

These kinds of people are invaluable during a time of weariness and discouragement. They lend refreshment through a word from God, a song, a card, a letter, or anointed preaching. They help give you the gusto to go forward again.

May God give to the church people such as this! Paul, who suffered much in weariness and painfulness (II Corinthians 11:27), was sent Onesiphorus to refresh him as stated in II Timothy:

> *The Lord give mercy unto the house of Onesiphorus; for he oft refreshed me, and was not ashamed of my chain: but, when he was in Rome, he sought me out very diligently, and found me* (II Timothy 1:16-17).

Onesiphorus went out of his way to help Paul. May we do the same for our brothers and sisters in the Lord!

NILAH K. MEAN

PASSING THE TORCH OF
BEING FAITHFUL TO THE CALL

While sitting at our dining room table this morning, glancing out the window with the maples, spruce, and pine trees showered with powdery white snow, munching on some good, home-cooked Red River cereal, along with wheat toast, strawberries, coffee, and tea, I began to reminisce about sixty-two years of ministry, which began at my first revival service in Madisonville, Kentucky.

The occasion was in a rented hall pastored by Opal Blackford. My pastor at Granite City, Illinois, was booked for this particular revival, but it was not possible for him to go because of certain demands at home. He came to me and said, "Nilah, I want you to go and preach that revival meeting." Since I was working at Walgreens Drugstore, I had to get permission to leave the job, which I did, and never went back.

My first revival meeting was fruitful with precious souls baptized in the all-saving name of Jesus and receiving the baptism of the Holy Ghost. I had found my true niche for my future. I was bursting at the seams with excitement and anticipation of God's will for my life.

God's call for my life went much farther back than this, while I lived on a yellow clay road in Roodhouse, Illinois. I was a member of the Llewellyn and Rose Rutledge family, and we lived on a ninety-three-acre farm in a humble five-room house. We walked two miles to school, which only had one room for all grades. Later I went to White Hall to attend high school and stayed with the Charles Rigdon family, who was pastor of the White Hall Pentecostal Church. Their son Calvin, whom I sparred and competed with during those years, later became the Conquerors' President of the UPC. Our eyes never met nor did we have any particular feeling for each other, just a part of the process in training for our future!

It was while living by the yellow clay road that my brother-in-law, Ressal Stoops, came home from work and exclaimed, "There's a holy-roller revival going on in the town of White Hall. What do you say that we all go?"

There were no seat-belt requirements in those days, so we all piled into that little Ford rumble-seated car and headed for town. Ruby Layel was the evangelist and was also an accomplished pianist, who inspired me to pursue the piano, and could she ever preach! Of course, our family being Baptist, we were awestruck by the fervor and anointing of God upon her life. When the altar call was given, I was one of the first to hit the altar. My dad started after me to take me away, being warned of what these Pentecostals might do to me. However, the rest of the family constrained him by saying, "Leave her alone. She will be all right." I was baptized in Jesus' name and received the Holy Ghost, and with this experience the call of God came into my life.

Right near our home was an old stump. That seemed to me like "holy ground." This is where I would go to pray. I can still remember Mom shouting, "Nilah! Hurry up with those vegetables. The men will be coming soon, and I want supper ready." However, when stopping by the old stump, I somehow seemed to forget my errand of getting the vegetables for supper as I would commune with my Lord, being awestruck by His presence—time went by so quickly. It seemed to me that these special times of waiting resulted in driving the call of God deeper and deeper into my spirit.

The ministry in the evangelistic field became more and more exciting. While I preached a meeting in Davenport, Iowa, a young lady came into the service whose expression seemed to portray a sincere yet somewhat of a desperate hunger for God. When the altar call was given she was in the altar.

With some help and direction she entered into a very beautiful relationship with the Lord. She was filled with the Holy Ghost and I had the joy of baptizing her in the Mississippi River in the all-saving name of Jesus Christ.

It was brought to my attention that this lady had narrowly escaped from a closed Carmelite convent, after twenty-two years of embarrassing, disappointing, and harrowing experiences. To put it plainly, she had received during this first night in the altar what she was desiring when entering the convent twenty-two years before.

To my next revival services Sister Charlotte came, and likewise the next. She was literally basking in the sunshine of a newfound life in the Lord Jesus.

One night I invited Charlotte to give her testimony. She did, and would you believe it, we continued to travel together for some fourteen years.

It would be interesting to have a survey across the continent to see the number of workers today who had their start in one of our revival services. One of the most prominent reasons why so many who came to God in our revival meetings continued to walk with God was definitely our doctrinal preaching. I would preach Jesus and His great salvation, which is vividly portrayed in the four Gospels, the Book of Acts as the door into God's great salvation, how the early church baptized, and what happened when they received the Holy Ghost. One statement we often made was "Some people pass up the Book of Acts, like a freight train does a bum!" I would stop for a moment and then chuckle. The point was getting through to them.

After preaching several nights about God's plan of getting into the church, I would preach what we referred to as "sinner sermons," such as "Seven Dips in a Muddy Pond" (the story of Naaman, the leper) or "Giving the Pigs a Permanent Wave" (the story of the prodigal son waving good-bye to return to his father). It worked!

Brother W. T. Stairs, the first Foreign Mission Secretary of the United Pentecostal Church (the office of Director was not yet established), heard us preach and invited us to come to the Maritime District to preach the first camp meeting on the new campsite in July 1952. During that time plans were also being made to crusade into the province of Nova Scotia with the apostolic message.

Brother Stairs invited us to preach the first revival meetings in this province following the camp meeting. We teamed up with the Lewis DeMerchant family, who were just recently brought into the apostolic message from a Baptist background, and John Mean, who was evangelizing in the district at that time.

The thrust into the province was made, resulting in a tent and Union Hall series of services. Twenty-eight were baptized in the name of Jesus Christ, and God began to outpour the power of the Holy Ghost. It was interesting indeed to return from our first crusade in Nova Scotia to the General Conference in Little Rock, Arkansas. There Sister Charlotte and I were ordained into the ministry. Brother A. T. Morgan was General Superintendent at that time.

The following year, we came back to preach the second camp in 1953. Following camp, we came again into Nova Scotia and did a crusade in another town. Wow! What a different experience this time. After the third night service, Sister Charlotte's testimony was getting too heavy for them to handle, so they gathered with a truckload of rocks and other instruments to drive us out of town. The mayor was there, trying to appease the anger but of course not favorable to us.

We had contacted the RCMP for protection, only to hear them say that they couldn't come into that town without an invitation from the mayor's office. Trenton, the town where we had pitched our tent, was connected to three other towns: New Glasgow, Stellarton, and Westphal. We stood for a time, just hesitating to make a decision, when Chief Langille of the New Glasgow Police Force came to us and said, "I see they're giving you a hard time. You come up to our town, and we'll look after you." So we decided to take the tent down, renting the IOOF Hall in New Glasgow. The revival continued and we began baptizing in the East River, and our God who is faithful began filling people with the Holy Ghost; so now there were two churches which had been started in Nova Scotia.

The third year was another exciting time. We were in the city of Halifax for a period of eight weeks. This capital city was very traditional in their religious beliefs; however, there were sixteen baptized in Jesus' precious name. A third church had now been started. The next year, we started another church in Truro. The following year, in 1956, we came again and did a crusade in the city of Dartmouth, situated across the harbor from Halifax.

One pattern we followed with each revival meeting was the placing of visitor cards in the hands of those who attended the services. On these was a place for their name, address, and phone number, along with the following two questions:

1. What is your church affiliation?
2. Would you like our pastor to call on you?

For every card that answered in the affirmative, we were on their doorstep within twenty-four hours. We always found that getting in the homes and discussing the doctrine were a plus in reaching them for the Lord.

During all this, John Mean and I were falling in love. It seemed that we were doing quite well in reaching the lost together, so we decided one day the most proper move would be to make our efforts binding so we married. Wow! Interesting! The contract we worked out was, "You come with me on the evangelistic field for one year, and we will return to Nova Scotia to continue our efforts of crusading new fields." Well, we had two years of beautiful experiences across the U.S.A., meeting many outstanding men and women of God, no negatives!

We returned in the summer of 1959 to the same campground, where we discussed with the brethren further pursuit into the province of Nova Scotia. Following camp we started to go to the Annapolis section of Nova Scotia; however, after parking the trailer for the night in the town of Amherst, we went out and walked on the streets and decided that since there was no Apostolic church in this town, we didn't really need to go further. So we rented the KP Hall, got the advertising out, and started another crusade.

Once again, God blessed us with some beautiful people being baptized and filled with the Holy Ghost. Another church had begun.

During the camp meeting before coming to Amherst we received some unfortunate news. While we were traveling through Phoenix, Arizona, we were advised that if we had any savings, it would be wise to deposit the same into Arizona Savings and Loan Company, which we did. While sitting in the camp meeting, we received word that our savings had gone down the drain. Ha!

The savings company had closed. We did have about $800 with us that we had accumulated from the sale of some 78- and 45-speed records we had made earlier. Remember, there was not a Home Missions program in those days, but our God was always sufficient. He was always there and on time—but never late. Hallelujah!

Having been in Amherst for approximately ten months, we felt God calling us back to Halifax. This was substantiated within a few days by our receiving a call from the church, since the minister then in charge planned to leave the pastorate in Halifax. We had a roof contractor whose wife had come into the church in Amherst and who, when learning we were returning to Halifax, offered to take our furniture in his truck. So we loaded our furniture on the truck, just reserving enough clothing and light articles to use over the following weekend, which included a fellowship rally on Monday, after which we would leave to take up the pastoral duties in Halifax.

We had traveled about one hundred miles towards Halifax, when all of a sudden smoke started pouring from the sides of the load. Ed pulled the truck over to the shoulder of the highway. I had our little budgie bird sitting on my lap in its cage. It was quite special in our house since we had taught it to talk. "Punkin is a pretty bird. Punkin is a Pentecostal bird, praise you, Jesus." Then it would say, "Goodness gracious, Punkin is a pretty, pretty, nasty bird, praise you, Jesus."

WORDS FROM JOHN MEAN

When the truck stopped, I ran in front of the truck approximately twenty or thirty feet, set the cage on the side of the road, then hurriedly ran back and climbed on top of the load and retrieved our bass viol. Ed took it and ran, placing it beside the budgie bird. I then began pulling a mattress from the top of the load; however, when the mattress was pulled clear, flames shot everywhere and we had to quickly abandon the vehicle. The police patrol was there shortly and ordered everyone back from the vehicle since the fire was burning close to the gas tank.

While we watched the fire burning literally all we owned, the fire grounded the starter in the engine and the motor started turning over and over. While the gearshift was in first gear and all brakes released, the truck rolled ahead just far enough to run over the bass viol and the budgie bird. One of the greatest lessons I ever learned was taught to me that day. In about two months we were expecting our first baby; I had bought Nilah a cedar chest lined with beautiful knotty pine on the outside. She had placed all the baby clothes inside this cedar chest. There was also a 30.06 rifle Nilah bought me, since we enjoyed the woods during deer season. Well, it all burned in a few minutes; however, while watching it all go up in flames, a sweet peace came over my soul as though the Holy Spirit enraptured my entire being. I expressed, "Thank you, Lord, for something precious you have placed in my soul that fire cannot destroy." We salvaged a broken coffee table and a rocking chair to set up housekeeping in Halifax.

God's people were so good that in less than two months we were given more than we lost. Brother E. L. Jacques, our District Superintendent, sent us his vacation pay envelope. God bless his memory.

We had not pastored in Halifax long when Nilah seemed to carry such an intense burden for the city of Dartmouth where we were living, just across the harbor from Halifax. We had just opened the work in Middleton from our work in Halifax, making the first payment on their new church lot through a penny drive sponsored by the ladies of the Halifax Church. Nilah's burden for Dartmouth refused to be restrained. One day she came into my office and said, "John, let's start a work in Dartmouth." I stood behind my desk, reached out and took her hand, and answered, "You get the money, and I'll do the building." She answered, "It's a deal!"

It sounds ridiculous; however, we accumulated a beautiful property and began building a church with no converts as yet. We posted a "For Sale" sign on our home, borrowed over $100,000, and went to work. That little lady went to the churches she had preached revivals for and challenged them to help plant a church in the needy city of Dartmouth. It was a long and exciting story, but to sum it up, our house sold. The church building progressed far enough for our family to move into some rooms at the rear of the church. Our oldest son, Nathan, boasted of having a larger bedroom than any boy in the city of Dartmouth had. When the crowd had left the service, Nathan would take his sleeping bag into the auditorium and sleep!

BACK TO NILAH MEAN

The dedication day came with our distinguished General Superintendent, Reverend and Mrs. N. A. Urshan, as special guest speakers. What a day of celebration and worship it was and with a packed house! The mayor of the city, Eileen Stubbs (which a short time later was baptized along with three of her daughters), was present to address the assembly. The next night, however, only eighteen people showed up for service. We were somewhat embarrassed, having such prominent speakers. Brother Urshan in his wisdom commented,

"Sister Nilah, don't you feel the least embarrassed. We understand what's going on."

I began preaching the first services of the revival services the following week, and souls began streaming to the altar. A black community east of the city of Dartmouth began coming in large numbers and asking, "Can we have this baptism of the Holy Ghost?" Of course, the answer as well as their experience was in the affirmative. What a glorious outpouring!

Week after week, we would be taking new converts to the church in Halifax to be baptized in Jesus' wonderful name.

In thirty days, when the first bank payment was due, the amount had come in. In five years, over $100,000 for the bank note, plus our house money, was repaid. The church was going and growing. To God be the glory! We had prison services, convalescent home services, street meetings, weekly home visitation, and you name it. We couldn't be a part of what God was doing and be idle. A man by the name of Robert Grady, who was a male nurse at the Nova Scotia Hospital, loved to sing and also provided delicious and sumptuous meals for the workers, especially on Saturday. On numerous occasions, he would prepare a great meal and invite all those who went on visitation to come and enjoy. Oh, the thrill to stop by Bob's apartment and eat while we shared our experiences of visitation that day!

One of the areas I believe that led in our initial growth was the high rate of involvement of the young people who continued to come to church. While they were undoubtedly made to feel welcome, I also believe that a large part of their feeling so welcome came about on account of my children. Even though they were fairly young when the church first opened—Nathan being fourteen, Kathy ten,

Pamela eight, and Steven six—their love of music and involvement and experimenting with musical groups, youth choirs, and generally involving all those who could carry a tune became the linchpin around which other young people gathered. While Nathan played the piano, Kathy would help him develop the choir lines for the sopranos. Likewise, Pam having a dusky voice far developed for her age would work out the alto. Steve began taking percussion lessons even at his age. By the time he was twelve, he was considered quite accomplished.

So it was that on Friday nights the youth choir would meet to practice. The youth choir was an exciting place to be. The kids would experiment with different tonal formation, different chord structures, all the while seeing just how interesting their harmony could become. The church loved it. Of those kids from North and East Preston who brought so much understanding of soul music to the choir, there were not just a few. With the various harmonies, rhythms, and experimentation of various styles and cultural coloratura being woven in order to produce the best sound and atmosphere possible, the excitement when they got up to sing could be electrifying. Bottom line: if you want your church to grow, have the kids of all ages take a leading role. Make church be a place where they can't wait to congregate, where music comes from the soul and creates electricity in the air. In such a place, empty seats will be harder and harder to find.

The church grew to the level where we were going to need a larger facility. A property just three blocks from us came up for sale. Since our church was located in a prime location and our street was the most reasonable access to several adjoining communities, we felt it was wise to stay on the same street; also, the statistics had it that 27,000 cars passed by daily. We placed an offer on the new property and got it for $185,000. Obviously, the many ramifications of building a new church building, the inflationary prices of materials, and working through the building codes and such at city hall were monumental in comparison with the building of our first churches. This would be a story all its own. We rejoice to tell you that on November 11, 2005, we dedicated our new facility.

During these years of getting off the ground, God blessed me with some very precious workers. In general my husband's church, Calvary Tabernacle, and all his saints made great sacrifice to see the existence of the Dartmouth church made possible; the work put in, the money given, the care and thoughtfulness of them all cannot be counted. In addition, Sister Linda Smith's church in downtown Halifax was helpful, especially in assisting in a time frame within which the second building came into fruition.

For several years starting in 1978, Brother Sam Cooper from Brother Kilgore's church in Houston, along with his wife Sandy, assisted me. He was a master of Sunday school organization and excitement! He was very adept at outreach.

Brother Mike Blume assisted me for several years afterwards. Not only was he of great assistance in ministerial activities, but also through his expertise, he was able to negotiate with a printing company in Hong Kong for the printing of my book, *From Convent to Pentecost,* about Sister Charlotte's life.

Helen Graves, one of the first converts in the work in Halifax, after graduating from U.P.B.I. in Fredericton, New Brunswick, returned home to Nova Scotia and lived with us some fourteen years. She helped me so graciously with our babies and growing family of four precious children. To this day our children think of her in special terms as one who gave herself so selflessly to their care.

In my failing health, having battled with Parkinson's disease for some twenty years, I prayed, "Lord, help me see the completion of this church before you call me home."

During the building of the new church, many friends came to our rescue at times we thought we had bitten off more than we could chew. I am constantly reminded of this great fellowship and of those who are so committed. What grand people of spirit who allow another's burden to become their own! To such loyalty I hope I will always be counted worthy. Any organization that houses within its ranks such people as Brother Kenneth Mendenhall of South Bend, Indiana, Brother Harry Lewis of Perth-Andover, New Brunswick, and the many others who came to us like angels sent from God, has an appreciation of greatness. So on the threshold of looking into that better place, I have come to the conclusion that those men and women I have known and with whom I have worked for more than sixty years are indeed the salt of the earth. I was not mistaken to put my faith in them. I do not find myself at the end of life's sojourn feeling embittered but having a calm belief that if I had it to do all over again, I would choose the same organization, the same friends, and definitely the same husband to embark upon the journey. What a life it has been!

The following business meeting, I turned over the torch of leadership to a man who had assisted my husband for some twenty years. His expertise in management and planning has already raised the church one step higher in our goal of reaching the city.

The following is the resolution that was presented to the congregation for consideration.

Resolution:

> *Whereas Eunilah Mean was founder and Pastor of the United Pentecostal Church of Dartmouth for some twenty-eight years, and whereas, the state of her health has diminished her ability to carry the full load of Pastoral responsibilities, and whereas, we still respect her admonition and wisdom in the decision-making process of our Assembly.*

Be it resolved:

> *That she would assume the role of Senior Pastor or Pastor Emerita.*

Be it further resolved:

> *That we elect a new Pastor to carry on the vision of the great Apostolic Church in the city of Dartmouth.*

It passed unanimously. The next action was the voting of a new pastor. Again, the vote for Brother James Underwood, who was with me for over one year, was unanimous.

In passing the torch, the following criteria were perused and considered.

1. Be sure the one resuming leadership will follow the same direction as its original purpose. Inasmuch as we realize we are only a part of what God is doing and not the whole, yet we need to feel quite confident that the apostolic message is heralded on high. Further, that there is no other name under heaven given among men, whereby we must be saved. We are a spiritual entity.

   O' what emphasis we must place upon a Holy

Spirit-filled and Holy Spirit-led life! The kingdom of God is within us. God uses our talents and abilities. There are times, however, when we need answers that we can't find in the textbooks. He always comes through and on time. Precious Jesus!

2. The beautiful message of His holiness must be proclaimed. When Balak sent for Balaam to curse Israel, he took him to three different vantage peaks to curse Israel. I often likened these three different places of observation to the three strong pillars of truth that keep God's people properly focused, (1) The name of the Lord, (2) the shekinah glory over the camp, and (3) holiness unto the Lord. It takes all three to receive our blessed Lord's approval and blessing.

   Inasmuch as we know the holy nature of our Lord is an impartation of His true nature to us, we humbly submit to Him "that [we might] show forth the praises of him who hath called [us] out of darkness into his marvellous light." (See I Peter 2:9.) What a privilege we women have of showing forth in our appearance and dress a sincere and godly witness for our Lord!

3. The oneness of the body cannot be impressed upon us too highly. Our concern one for another is the heartbeat of our Lord. Yea! Many are the epitaphs of those who were self-seekers rather than being compassionate for the oneness of the body. May God help us to humble ourselves and submit one to another even if we cannot fully comprehend the point. Hang in there; the light will come shining through someday and you will be glad you did.

4. Finances is another area of concern, that is, our

attitude toward finances, when passing the torch. If you are in the ministry for the monetary gain or easy living, "forget it." It seems I read somewhere where God said He would supply all our need, according to His riches in glory! Is your God rich? Mine is. Then why worry? It also seems as though I've read where our heavenly Father even observes the sparrows fall and then challenges us with His observation and evaluation of us as being of much more worth than many sparrows. In the space of well over fifty years of ministry, I've never asked for a penny, that is, for myself, but God did supply. Oh yes! I could write a book about God's provisions.

We must be good stewards, however, of every penny. You see, they are God's provisions, and He is faithful. Make sure your meditations upon the dollar are not about scanning the stock market but rather about being safely deposited into heaven's bank. The interest gains are unimaginable. Wow!

5. We expect the one who takes up our torch to understand the true value of prayer. Since the church's historical book of the New Testament mentions prayer as many times as it has chapters, this should be sufficient guide for us to perk up our ears and get the message.

   Prayer is like a partnership; it's a sharing with the one who understands we move together with Him. Mark 16:20 says, "They went forth, and preached every where, the Lord working with them, and confirming the word with signs following." We can't leave Him behind in any of our endeavors. We must spend quality time in communion each day and then travel together.

6. Inasmuch as waiting in His presence is important, we must arise to the work. Jesus said, "I must work the works of him that sent me, while it is day." We must go to the next town and the next; we must pray. Then we must get up and get with it. We can't sit around hoping for souls to come. We must go after them.
7. We must prepare for this time of passing the torch by training others in places of responsibilities. This can be quite a normal procedure if we plan for the change soon enough; otherwise, there may arise certain difficulties if the dedication of the one who takes the torch is not in sync with the heartbeat of the one passing it.

   It seems to be biblical procedure that the one passing the torch was very careful to place it into the proper hands that would carry on the same vision of the one who passed it to them.

   For example: the apostle Paul to Timothy, his son in the faith (II Timothy 3:14-17; 4:1-8). Also, another church, that of Galatia, he was instrumental in raising up but was later worried about those who had come in among them, preaching what the apostle termed as "another gospel." In this case, it was the Judaizers who shouted that the followers of Christ must also keep the ordinances of the law in order to be saved. The apostle answered, "If I build again the things which I destroyed, I make myself a transgressor," and "If any man preach any other gospel [than I have preached] . . . , let him be accursed" (Galatians 2:18; 1:6-9).
8. Still another elder wrote in I Peter 5:1-4 to the elders, "I exhort, who am also an elder . . . feed

the flock of God," over whom the Holy Ghost hath made you overseer. It's amazing how some seem to get more pleasure out of fleecing the flock than feeding them. Just a word to the wise: You only fleece the flock once each year; however, they must be fed every day.

A BRIEF OBSERVATION FROM JOHN MEAN

Perhaps the one thing that stands out more than anything about Eunilah K. (Rutledge) Mean is her positivism. There is not a negative bone in her whole being. If she felt it was the will of God, she pursued it with fervor. She not only believed it would happen; she got involved and made it happen.

Furthermore, her leadership was not one of demanding but rather, "Come and go with me, and we will share together and see what God can do." My mind wanders to a very exciting experience along a lonely tributary of the Amazon River. We had just come in from an alligator hunt (successful). Brother Bennie DeMerchant screwed our hammocks to the wall, and we all climbed in for a good night's sleep. Nilah spoke across the room to Brother DeMerchant and asked about any needs they might have that we might help them with back home. He answered by mentioning the need for workers, adding that they were only able to send about three students to Rio to the Bible school each year. Nilah answered back, "Bennie DeMerchant, you're doing things wrong!" He answered, "What do you mean?" Nilah then quipped, "Start your own Bible school." Things went silent for a few seconds and then Brother DeMerchant answered, "That's what I'm going to do." There could be others facing the same plight who could follow Brother DeMerchant's example. What a blessing it would be!

It was interesting to receive a letter from the DeMerchants a few years ago to tell us there were over one thousand students enrolled in their Bible school program that year. Then he made a gesture to the effect of "You planted the seed thought in my mind that night in the humble cottage in the jungle."

10

Mantle of Character

BY JOY HANEY

Through the years I've heard character described as this: "Character is what you are in the dark, when no one is looking." Churches can be increased or decreased by the character of its leaders. During our time of being pastor of Christian Life Center, we brought on our staff a young man and his wife to be our youth leaders. Little things started happening that were not quite right, and finally my husband knew that he had to let them go. Later a certain businessman in the city told him that this young man did not pay his bills.

What we are has an effect upon the church and is a witness in the community. Either it says something about the character of Christ who lives inside of us, or it lets them know that He does not.

It has been said, "What you are speaks so loud I can't hear what you're saying."

One of the first things in having good character is to hate evil and love good as stated in Proverbs 8:13: "The fear of the LORD is to hate evil: pride, and arrogancy, and the evil way, and the froward mouth, do I hate."

Matthew Henry says,

> Wherever there is an awe of God there is a dread of sin, as an evil. Conceit of ourselves, pride, and arrogance are sins which Christ hates, and so do all those who have the Spirit of Christ. The forward mouth, peevishness towards others, God hates, because it is such an enemy to the peace of mankind, and therefore we should hate it.

When there is an awe of God, there seems to be more of an understanding spirit towards others. As God is enlarged in the vision, prideful and mean spirits are diminished. That is why we are told to be *filled* with the Spirit in Ephesians 3:19: "And to know the love of Christ, which passeth knowledge, that ye might be filled with all the fulness of God."

When we are filled with Him, then our desires will be right and our consciences will be pricked when we do something that does not please Him. We will walk in newness of life and will live the blessed life. It is important to live in such a way that we can please God and live with a good conscience as the following paragraph states:

> Spend your time in nothing which you know must be repented of; in nothing on which you might not pray the blessing of God; in nothing which you could not review with a quiet conscience on your dying bed; in nothing which you might not safely and properly be found doing if death should surprise you in the act.
>
> —RICHARD BAXTER[19]

Character is what you are inside. The goal of life is to grow into the likeness of Christ and let His character become part of you. To live in such a way that others are lifted just by being in one's presence is the ultimate compliment to anyone. The following poem expresses it well:

TOUCHING SHOULDERS

There's a comforting thought at the close of the
day,
When I'm weary and lonely and sad,
That sort of grips hold of this crusty old heart
And bids it be merry and glad.
It gets in my soul, and drives out the blues
And finally thrills though and through.
It is just a sweet memory that chants the
refrain,
I'm glad I touched shoulders with you.
Did you know you were brave, did you know
you were strong?
Did you know there was one leaning hard?
Did you know that I waited and listened and
prayed?
And was cheered by your simplest word?
Did you know that I longed for that smile on
your face?
For the sound of your voice ringing true?
Did you know I grew stronger, and better
because
I had merely rubbed shoulders with you?

— AUTHOR UNKNOWN[20]

Everyone will have moments when anger comes and tempers flare, but learning to have control of the negative emotions is part of growing a good character. This means that someone has learned to control his spirit as stated in

Proverbs 16:32: "He that is slow to anger is better than the mighty; and he that ruleth his spirit than he that taketh a city."

Proverbs 14:29 further states: "He that is slow to wrath is of great understanding: but he that is hasty of spirit exalteth folly."

This verse of Scripture is proven in the story of Abigail. Her husband's name was Nabal, and he was churlish and evil in his ways. When his men were in the fields with their flocks, David and his men had been their protectors, so David sent messengers to Nabal asking for food. When Nabal received the request, he said, "Who is David?" Nabal was arrogant and refused to give anything to David.

When David heard this, he buckled on his sword and had his men do likewise. David said, "I'll show him who David is." With blood in his eye and vengeance on his mind, he and his four hundred men started toward Nabal's house.

One of the young servants of Nabal went to Nabal's wife and told her what was happening. She knew that this would hurt David's chances of becoming king, so she determined to stop him. She, without her husband knowing, ordered two hundred loaves of bread, the meat of five sheep, and five measures of parched corn, one hundred clusters of raisins, and two hundred cakes of figs, along with two bottles of wine, to be put on asses, and she made haste to go to David.

When she reached him, she fell before David on her face and bowed herself to the ground and said, "Upon me, my lord, upon me let this iniquity be: and let thine handmaid, I pray thee, speak in thine audience, and hear the words of thine handmaid" (I Samuel 25:24).

She went on to tell him not to regard Nabal,

because he had acted foolishly. Then she reminded David that he was not to shed blood, because when he came into the kingship it would be a grief unto him. David said to her,

> *Blessed be the* LORD *God of Israel, which sent thee this day to meet me: and blessed be thy advice, and blessed be thou, which hast kept me this day from coming to shed blood, and from avenging myself with mine own hand* (I Samuel 25:32-33).

I Samuel 25:3 describes Abigail:

> *Now the name of the man was Nabal; and the name of his wife Abigail: and she was a woman of good understanding, and of a beautiful countenance: but the man was churlish and evil in his doings*

She was described as a woman of good understanding. Proverbs 13:15 states, "Good understanding giveth favour." Abigail certainly secured the favor of David. When her husband died ten days after he uttered the words, "Who is David?" David sent word to Abigail that he wanted her to be his wife.

How does one develop good character and good understanding? This is answered by the following statement:

> The study of God's word, for the purpose of discovering God's will, is the secret discipline which has formed the greatest characters.
>
> —J. W. ALEXANDER[21]

How can the Word of God help form good character?

The following verses of Sripture are just a few reasons:

Proverbs 30:5: "Every word of God is pure: he is a shield unto them that put their trust in him."

The purity of His Word is planted in the mind.

Luke 8:11: "The seed is the word of God."

That seed of thought germinates and flourishes into action.

I Peter 1:23: "Being born again . . . by the word of God, which liveth and abideth for ever."

We become new in our thinking, which affects our character.

I John 2:14: "The word of God abideth in you, and ye have overcome the wicked one."

We overcome bad character because the Word of God in the heart dictates our actions.

Psalm 119:11: "Thy word have I hid in mine heart, that I might not sin against thee."

Hidden from view is a gold mine of thought obtained from the treasure house of His Word.

Psalm 119:105: "Thy word is a lamp unto my feet, and a light unto my path."

Lights go on in the brain, and lamps are lit in the heart that illuminate our thinking processes.

Psalm 119:130: "The entrance of thy words giveth light; it giveth understanding unto the simple."

We become women of understanding, surprising ourselves at the nuggets God gives us.

Psalm 119:133: "Order my steps in thy word: and let not any iniquity have dominion over me."

Our character is dominated by His Word, which is reflected in our choice of steps.

Hebrews 4:12: "For the word of God is quick, and powerful, and sharper than any twoedged sword, piercing even to the dividing asunder of soul and spirit, and of the joints and marrow, and is a discerner of the thoughts and intents of the heart."

There it is. The Word is a light which gives understanding. It keeps you from sin. The pureness of His Word helps disinfect wrong thinking. We are made new every day by the washing of the Word. His Word orders our steps because we are listening to a *voice of power* other than our own. His Word goes into the thought processes and cuts off that which is not like Christ and replaces it with His higher thoughts.

There is a Chinese proverb that states the following: "If there is righteousness in the heart, there is beauty in the character. If there is beauty in the character, there will be harmony in the home. If there is harmony in the home, there will be order in the nation. When there is order in the nation, there will be peace in the world."

It all starts with righteousness and the beauty of character.

No matter what the situation, anyone can develop good character if they so desire. This was exemplified in the story of Abigail, who lived with a man of evil character, and is demonstrated also in the famous Russian author, Leo Tolstoy, as the following story depicts:

> A good many years ago there was born in Russia a boy who thought himself so ugly that he felt there was no happiness for such as he. He had a wide nose, thick lips, small grey eyes, and big hands and feet. When he grew to be a man he became a famous writer. In one of his books he tells that he was so anxious about this ugliness that he besought God to work a miracle, to turn

him into a beauty. If God would do this the boy promised that he would give God all he then possessed, or would possess in the future.

That Russian boy was the great Count Tolstoi. Happily, as he grew older he discovered that the beauty for which he sighed was not the only beauty, nor the best beauty. He learned to value more the beauty of a character strong and great and good in God's sight.

—James Hastings[22]

THE INTEGRITY OF THE TONGUE

Proverbs 11:3 says, "The integrity of the upright shall guide them: but the perverseness of transgressors shall destroy them."

Proverbs 15:4 also talks about perverseness: "A wholesome tongue is a tree of life: but perverseness therein is a breach in the spirit."

Perverseness is usually expressed by way of the tongue. Proverbs 17:20 expresses this: "He that hath a perverse tongue falleth into mischief."

Notice how integrity and perverseness are talked about in Proverbs 19:1: "Better is the poor that walketh in his integrity, than he that is perverse in his lips, and is a fool."

In the above verses of Scripture one word is continually talked about: perverseness. What does it mean to be perverse? Three words were found to describe perverse: wicked, stubborn, contrary. Under those words were the following words: vicious, mean, rebellious, unreasonable, difficult, and bad.

So it is our choice to have a wholesome tongue which is as a tree of life or a perverse tongue which brings the hearer down, as well as those who speak perverse things.

The better choice would be to have a good tongue which is healing, not a perverse tongue which wounds and is spiteful and abusive.

Our mouth can cause or create problems, or it can bring peace and joy as stated in Proverbs 15:23: "A man hath joy by the answer of his mouth: and a word spoken in due season, how good is it!"

The following poem says it well:

CHOOSE CAREFULLY

A careless word may kindle strife;
A cruel word may wreck a life.
A bitter word may hate instill;
A brutal word may smite and kill.

A gracious word may smooth the way;
A joyous word may light the day.
A timely word may lessen stress;
A loving word may heal and bless.

– AUTHOR UNKNOWN[23]

KEEP YOUR TONGUE FROM SPEAKING EVIL

This is a sign of good character. People reveal what is inside them by what they speak. If there is envy in the heart, it will manifest itself by trying to shed a bad light on someone else. In the following verses the apostle Paul instructed us to put away evil speaking:

Titus 3:2: "To speak evil of no man, to be no brawlers, but gentle, shewing all meekness unto all men."

Ephesians 4:31: "Let all bitterness, and wrath, and anger, and clamour, and evil speaking, be put away from you, with all malice."

Minister's wives have enough trouble trying to keep

everything together without being stabbed by the tongue of a fellow minister's wife. It is bad character to spread things that hurt other people. In fact, in Proverbs 10:18 God calls the person who does this a fool: "He that uttereth a slander, is a fool."

Evil words that tear down, cast shadows on a person's character, or separate friends hurt. Proverbs 18:8 describes this: "The words of a talebearer are as wounds, and they go down into the innermost parts of the belly."

It is best to pray about a matter instead of spreading something that causes grief, embarrassment, and pain. The blessing is upon those who *conceal* rather than *reveal* as stated in Proverbs 11:13: "A talebearer revealeth secrets: but he that is of a faithful spirit concealeth the matter."

God calls those who conceal a matter faithful. That is the highest compliment from Him, as that is what will be spoken when we enter into heaven, "Well done, thou good and faithful servant. Enter thou into the joy of thy Lord."

Therefore, we must teach our mouths how to speak so we can be spiritually and physically healthy as stated in the following verses of Scripture:

Proverbs 16:23: "The heart of the wise teacheth his mouth, and addeth learning to his lips."

Proverbs 16:24: "Pleasant words are as an honeycomb, sweet to the soul, and health to the bones."

GOOD PRINCIPLES

When President James A. Garfield was a youth, an elderly friend gave him a set of personal principles that he cherished to the end of life. We could learn from them also. The guide read:

Never be idle.
Make few promises.
Always speak the truth.
Live within your income.
Never speak evil of anyone.
Keep good company or none.
Live up to your engagements.
Never play games of chance.
Drink no intoxicating drinks.
Good character is above everything else.
Keep your own secrets if you have any.
Never borrow if you can possibly help it.
When you speak to a person look into his eyes.
Save when you are young to spend when you are old.
Never run into debt unless you see a way out again.
Good company and good conversation are the sinews of virtue.
Your character cannot be essentially injured except by your own acts.
If anybody speaks evil of you let your life be so that no one believes him.
When you retire at night think over what you have done during the day.
If your hands cannot be employed usefully, attend to the culture of your mind.
Read the above carefully and thoughtfully at least once a week.[24]

Good principles help develop good character. Seek to live your life so that those who follow you will be influenced for the good. Honesty, faithfulness, kindness, loyalty, integrity, diligence, no matter what it may be, always choose to take the higher road of living and let your life shine.

In his "Idylls of the King," Tennyson gives the knight's pledge:

> Live pure, speak truth, right the wrong, follow the king; else wherefore born?
>
> Is not this a good motto for the Christian? He [she] must live a pure life, which means a holy one; he [she] certainly must speak the truth and do what he [she] can to right conditions that are wrong. Above all, he [she] must follow the King, the Lord Jesus Christ, the Author and Finisher of our faith.[25]

MORAL PURITY

> *He that is unjust, let him be unjust still: and he which is filthy, let him be filthy still: and he that is righteous, let him be righteous still: and he that is holy, let him be holy still* (Revelation 22:11).

There is a distinction between filthiness of the flesh and holiness of the spirit. Jesus continues in Revelation 22:12 and says that every man will be rewarded by how he chose to live: "And, behold, I come quickly; and my reward is with me, to give every man according as his work shall be."

In an age where there is much moral decline, there is an unequivocal need for moral purity. Clear, unmistakable standards of morality are necessary to this generation that is so bent on practicing filthy living by God's standards.

What God says is immoral is still immoral no matter that some of society tries to state otherwise. God's Word is still the plumb line for proper living and actions. Fornication, adultery, homosexuality, and lesbianism will not enter into heaven:

But the fearful, and unbelieving, and the abominable, and murderers, and whoremongers, and sorcerers, and idolaters, and all liars, shall have their part in the lake which burneth with fire and brimstone: which is the second death (Revelation 21:8).

The following verses of Scripture will judge mankind at the judgment:

Whoremongers and the abominable will both perish in the fire. *Whoremongers* are those who sin sexually by such acts as adultery and fornication. *Abominable* is associated with homosexuality as the following verses of Scripture indicate:

Leviticus 18:22: "Thou shalt not lie with mankind, as with womankind: it is abomination."

Romans 1:26-27: "For this cause God gave them up unto vile affections: for even their women did change the natural use into that which is against nature: and likewise also the men, leaving the natural use of the woman, burned in their lust one toward another; men with men working that which is unseemly, and receiving in themselves that recompence of their error which was meet."

Leviticus 20:13: "If a man also lie with mankind, as he lieth with a woman, both of them have committed an abomination: they shall surely be put to death; their blood shall be upon them."

It is unnatural for men to lie with men and commit sexual acts, the same as it is for women to do likewise. It is vile and abominable to God. For this they will be cast into the fire of hell if there is not repentance made.

Leviticus also condemns adultery and fornication:

> *And the man that committeth adultery with another man's wife, even he that committeth adultery with his neighbour's wife, the adulterer and the adulteress shall surely be put to death. And the man that lieth with his father's wife hath uncovered his father's nakedness: both of them shall surely be put to death; their blood shall be upon them. And if a man lie with his daughter in law, both of them shall surely be put to death: they have wrought confusion; their blood shall be upon them* (Leviticus 20:10-12).

Death was the penalty for adultery and fornication in the Old Testament. In the New Testament it was still regarded as evil, but the death penalty of the Old Testament is now put at the end of one's life, not at the immediate moment. God never did change His laws on adultery and fornication, but His grace makes it possible not to die but to live if the guilty one repents and lives right.

The works of the flesh and their judgments are listed in Galatians:

> *Now the works of the flesh are manifest, which are these; Adultery, fornication, uncleanness, lasciviousness, idolatry, witchcraft, hatred, variance, emulations, wrath, strife, seditions, heresies, envyings, murders, drunkenness, revellings, and such like: of the which I tell you before, as I have also told you in time past, that they which do such things shall not inherit the kingdom of God* (Galatians 5:19-21).

If we know what God likes and what He doesn't, then we need to walk according to His way and not live a life of infidelity that leads to despair. For this is what happens when one follows the way of the flesh: anything goes (no standards, no disciplines or purity), life becomes unbearable, and unhappiness is the result. There is no fulfillment in sin!

Every day it is essential to take a spiritual bath and let the clean Spirit of Jesus wash away any thoughts that cause temptations to take up residence in the mind that would cause a separation from Him.

To live a disciplined life of moral purity is essential to be able to let the pure light of Jesus shine through us. As Jesus is the principal person who lives in our hearts, then there is no room for anything that would offend His purity. The temple that we have erected for Him should be daily swept clean and made a holy place for His presence to permeate. This leaves no room for suggestive literature to influence us; neither should there be any room in our lives for pornography or anything as demeaning. God help us to run from this filth! Never even peek at it. Flee from it as you would a rattlesnake. Shady actions and anything that we allow into our lives that would lead to self-destruction should not be allowed.

It is like the story told of a passenger on board a plane bound from Zurich to Beirut before the stringent security measures were installed. While flying, he cried out that he was suffocating. The plane landed at Athens, and Joseph Pasatour was taken to a hospital, where he died. Undressing him, hospital attendants discovered that he was a smuggler and had on a corset with 1,500 valuable Swiss watches. Closer examination revealed that the contraband merchandise had restricted his breathing and caused his death.

This is exactly what sin and moral impurity do. The sins that people try to hide from others actually suffocate the pure life of Christ out of them. The price is not worth the sin.

Dirty walls in our minds where thought pictures hang, dirty rooms where unwanted characters reside, dirty thoughts need a Holy Ghost spring cleaning. They need to be scrubbed with the brush of the Holy Writ (Psalm 119:9), sprayed with fuller's soap (Malachi 3:2), and watered down with rivers of living water (John 7:38). Get rid of everything that is debilitating and that shackles you. It is time to be free! This is demonstrated in David's prayer and plea for forgiveness. He asked God to give him a clean heart, and then he said in Psalm 51:12: "Restore unto me the joy of thy salvation; and uphold me with thy free spirit." There is a freedom that comes from living right.

Not only is there liberty in Christ's way, but it is commanded that those who bear the vessels of the Lord are to be clean. We are bearers of His gospel to a world that is filled with sin; therefore, we should have clean hearts and hands that stand in Christ's stead. Isaiah 52:11 states: "Be ye clean, that bear the vessels of the LORD."

There was once a young boy who wanted to help his mother as she prepared the evening meal. Often he would ask her, "Mother, may I put the bread on the table?" She would always reply, "My son, are your hands clean?" Years later he was called to be a preacher, and even though his mother had passed on, he could still hear her voice, "My son, are your hands clean?"

Christ asks the church this question today, "My sons and daughters, are your hearts and hands clean that handle the Bread of Life?" We are made clean through Jesus: His blood, His Word, and His Spirit as stated in the following verses of Scripture:

His Blood:

I John 1:7: "But if we walk in the light, as he is in the light, we have fellowship one with another, and the blood of Jesus Christ his Son cleanseth us from all sin."

Revelation 1:5: "And from Jesus Christ, who is the faithful witness, and the first begotten of the dead, and the prince of the kings of the earth. Unto him that loved us, and washed us from our sins in his own blood."

His Word:

John 15:3: "Now ye are clean through the word which I have spoken unto you."

Ephesians 5:26: "That he might sanctify and cleanse it [church] with the washing of water by the word."

His Spirit:

Titus 3:5: "Not by works of righteousness which we have done, but according to his mercy he saved us, by the washing of regeneration, and renewing of the Holy Ghost."

I Corinthians 6:11: "And such were some of you: but ye are washed, but ye are sanctified, but ye are justified in the name of the Lord Jesus, and by the Spirit of our God."

Jesus made a way for us to be morally pure. I John 1:9 declares it: "If we confess our sins, he is faithful and just to forgive us our sins, and to cleanse us from all unrighteousness."

There is true joy to those who serve God with their whole heart, but misery to those who serve Him half-heartedly as the following discourse depicts:

> This is the only way to find fullness of joy,—complete, unconditional surrender to

God. "Yield yourselves unto God." There is no very great measure of joy in a half-hearted Christian life. Many so-called Christians have just "enough religion to make them miserable." They can no longer enjoy the world and they have not entered into the "joy of the Lord."

-R. A. TORREY[26]

11

Mantle of Love

BY JOY HANEY

Jesus emphasized the subject of *love* in many of His discourses. He stated in John:

> *A new commandment I give unto you, That ye love one another; as I have loved you, that ye also love one another. By this shall all men know that ye are my disciples, if ye have love one to another* (John 13:34-35).

Love never tears down another to lift self, neither does it try to wound someone or insert a suspicious thought in the mind of one person about another. Love is bigger than that and is kind.

The mantle of love that is being talked about is the love that first began at Calvary, a love that was willing to give until it hurt, even for those who cried, "Crucify Him, crucify Him!" There have been those in every generation who have kept this love alive and have caused true love to be preserved even until now. The only way to judge true love is to measure it against the biblical definition of love given in I Corinthians 13:4-8, listed below:

- Love is longsuffering and is kind.
- Love envies not.
- Love does not vaunt itself nor is puffed up.
- Loves does not behave itself in an unseemly manner.
- Love is not easily provoked.
- Love thinks no evil.
- Love rejoiceth not in iniquity.
- Love rejoices in truth.
- Love bears all things.
- Love believes all things.
- Love hopes for all things.
- Love endures all things.
- Love never fails.

Jesus, who was love, gave a profound object lesson of what love should be when He was in the Garden of Gethsemane with His disciples. Judas approached Jesus and said, "Hail, master," and kissed him. "And Jesus said unto him, Friend, wherefore art thou come?" (Matthew 26:50).

Jesus did not disown Judas or treat him rudely, but He called him *friend*. This is the most amazing example of love. Jesus did not condone what Judas did; neither did He condemn him. He simply called him *friend*.

I Peter 4:8 emphasizes that this kind of love is *above all*: "And above all things have fervent charity among yourselves: for charity shall cover the multitude of sins."

Love is not blind—it sees more, not less.
But because it sees more, it is willing to see less.

—Rabbi Julius Gordon[27]

LOVE YOUR NEIGHBOR AS YOURSELF

This is the second greatest commandment as stated in Mark 12:31: "And the second is like, namely this, Thou shalt love thy neighbour as thyself. There is none other commandment greater than these."

Your neighbor is anyone, whether they are personal friends or complete strangers. Jesus proved this in the story of the Good Samaritan. A lawyer tried to tempt Jesus by talking about the two greatest commandments, and after Jesus told him, the lawyer asked, "And who is my neighbour?" (Luke 10:29).

That is when Jesus told the story about how the Samaritan helped the man who had been beaten and robbed, but the priest and the Levite did not. Then Jesus asked the lawyer, "Which now of these three, thinkest thou, was neighbour unto him that fell among the thieves?" (Luke 10:36).

"And he said, He that shewed mercy on him. Then said Jesus unto him, Go, and do thou likewise" (Luke 10:37).

This proves that anyone who has a need is our neighbor. We should be careful how we treat people. When we treat them with love, we are really ministering to the Lord Jesus.

God keeps record of our acts of love as stated in Proverbs 19:17: "He that hath pity upon the poor lendeth unto the LORD; and that which he hath given will he pay him again."

When we ignore or laugh at those in need, we are mocking our Lord as described in Proverbs 17:5: "Whoso mocketh the poor reproacheth his Maker."

It is our duty to lift up the fallen, be kind to the undeserving, show love to anyone who is in need; therefore, is Christ's love made manifest.

Jesus said in Matthew:

> *Ye have heard that it hath been said, Thou shalt love thy neighbour, and hate thine enemy. But I say unto you, Love your enemies, bless them that curse you, do good to them that hate you, and pray for them which despitefully use you, and persecute you. . . . For if ye love them which love you, what reward have ye? do not even the publicans the same?* (Matthew 5:43-44, 46).

True love is described in the following paragraph:

> Loving means to love that which is unlovable, or it is no virtue at all; forgiving means to pardon the unpardonable, or it is no virtue at all; faith means believing the unbelievable, or it is no virtue at all. And to hope means hoping when things are hopeless, or it is no virtue at all.
>
> —GILBERT K. CHESTERTON[28]

This is the concept on which we built the congregation in Stockton, California, Christian Life Center. It did not matter *who* they were, *where* they came from, or *what* they had done; we loved them. The fallen, the strange, the lonely, the poor, the rich, the talented, it did not matter who they were; we loved them all. By loving them we accepted them, included them, and made them feel important, that they belonged. In loving them we found God's favor. The more we loved, the more people God sent for us to love.

LOVE ONE ANOTHER

Jesus commanded His disciples in John 15:12 to love one another: "This is my commandment, That ye love one another, as I have loved you." He further stated in John 15:14 that those who do this become His friends: "Ye are my friends, if ye do whatsoever I command you."

Loving one another is the fulfillment of the law as stated in Roman 13:8: "But to love one another: for he that loveth another hath fulfilled the law."

I John 3:11 reiterates this doctrine: "For this is the message that ye heard from the beginning, that we should love one another."

A life without love for one another is like a dead fire and a cold heap of ashes. No light, no life, nothing but blackness. We need one another.

> *Two are better than one; because they have a good reward for their labour. For if they fall, the one will lift up his fellow: but woe to him that is alone when he falleth; for he hath not another to help him up* (Ecclesiastes 4:9-10).

We need to help and encourage each other in this short life, for what we do now will affect eternity. While we have a chance, let us love one another as the following paragraph says so well:

> I'm going your way, so let us go hand in hand. You help me and I'll help you. We shall not be here very long, for soon death, the kind old nurse, will come back and rock us all to sleep. Let us help one another while we may.
>
> —William Morris[29]

GOD IS LOVE

Love comes from God. He only is love.

Riches take wings, comforts vanish, hope withers away, but love stays with us. God is love.

—LEW WALLACE[30]

Beloved, let us love one another: for love is of God; and every one that loveth is born of God, and knoweth God. He that loveth not knoweth not God; for God is love. . . . Beloved, if God so loved us, we ought also to love one another. No man hath seen God at any time. If we love one another, God dwelleth in us, and his love is perfected in us (I John 4:7-8, 11-12).

Part of showing God's love is to obey Matthew 7:1: "Judge not, that ye be not judged." The following poem depicts this:

JUDGE NOT

Pray, find no fault with the man who limps,
Or stumbles along the road;
Unless you have worn the shoes he wears
Or struggled beneath his load.

There may be tacks in his shoes that hurt,
Though hidden away from view:
Or the burdens he bears, placed on your back
Might cause you to stumble, too.

Don't sneer at the man who's down today
Unless you have felt the blow
That caused his fall, or felt the shame
That only the fallen know.

You may be strong, but still the blows
That were his, if dealt to you,
In the selfsame way at the selfsame time,
Might cause you to falter too.[31]

When the scribes and Pharisees brought a woman taken in adultery to Jesus, they asked, "Master, this woman was taken in adultery, in the very act. Now Moses in the law commanded us, that such should be stoned: but what sayest thou?" (John 8:4-5).

They were ready to kill her, but Jesus, who came not to condemn but to save, simply ignored them, stooped down, and with His finger wrote on the ground. Then He answered them, "He that is without sin among you, let him first cast a stone at her" (John 8:7).

What did He write? Some say it was the secret sins of those who accused her. Whatever it was, love triumphed over the law. After all the men quietly disappeared, Jesus turned to the woman and said to her,

> *Woman, where are those thine accusers? hath no man condemned thee? She said, No man, Lord. And Jesus said unto her, Neither do I condemn thee: go, and sin no more* (John 8:10-11).

Our mission of love should be His:

> *The Spirit of the Lord is upon me, because he hath anointed me to preach the gospel to the poor; he hath sent me to heal the brokenhearted, to preach deliverance to the captives, and recovering of sight to the blind, to set at liberty them that are bruised* (Luke 4:18).

This is love! To give until it hurts, to believe in someone until they are delivered, to lift up the downtrodden, to bind up the brokenhearted, to do all the things that Christ came to earth to do, and then the ultimate sacrifice of love: to lay His life down and die so that the world might be saved.

He was crucified, died, and was buried, but He rose from the dead and now lives triumphantly.

> The world cannot bury Christ. The earth is not deep enough for his tomb, the clouds are not wide enough for his winding-sheet; he ascends into the heavens, but the heavens cannot contain him. He still lives in the church which burns unconsumed with his love; in the truth that reflects his image; in the hearts which flame with his love; in the spirit which is infused with his power.[32]

Let us burn unconsumed with His love. May our churches be healing centers, and may the downtrodden come and be lifted into victory! May the love of God erase our prejudice, our pettiness, and strife! Let us be marked by His love.

Let love be the banner that is unfurled over us as Song of Solomon 2:4 states: "He brought me to the banqueting house, and his banner over me was love." Let this love identify us to the world that we truly love like our Master loves.

12

Mantle of the Supernatural

By Joy Haney and Elsie Lund

JOY HANEY

In a negative world that is filled with disaster and daily crisis, it is easy for the spirit of the world to rub off on the church, but this should not be. We must contend for the faith that was once delivered to the church, not only the doctrines but also the supernatural power that is resident in a Spirit-filled believer and in the church.

The Book of Acts is filled with the signs and wonders of the early church. The miracles are what caused many to believe in Jesus and His gospel, as the following instances portray:

Acts 2:43: "And fear came upon every soul: and many wonders and signs were done by the apostles."

Acts 3:7 gives the miracle of the lame man: "And he [Peter] took him by the right hand, and lifted him up: and immediately his feet and ancle bones received strength."

Acts 5:12, 14-16: "And by the hands of the apostles were many signs and wonders wrought among the people;

(and they were all with one accord in Solomon's porch. . . . And believers were the more added to the Lord, multitudes both of men and women.) Insomuch that they brought forth the sick into the streets, and laid them on beds and couches, that at the least the shadow of Peter passing by might overshadow some of them. There came also a multitude out of the cities round about unto Jerusalem, bringing sick folks, and them which were vexed with unclean spirits: and they were healed every one."

Acts 8:5-7: "Then Philip went down to the city of Samaria, and preached Christ unto them. And the people with one accord gave heed unto those things which Philip spake, hearing and seeing the miracles which he did. For unclean spirits, crying with loud voice, came out of many that were possessed with them: and many taken with palsies, and that were lame, were healed."

Acts 9:41-42 shows that Tabitha was raised from the dead: "And he [Peter] gave her his hand, and lifted her up, and when he had called the saints and widows, presented her alive. And it was known throughout all Joppa; and many believed in the Lord."

Acts 14:8-10: "And there sat a certain man at Lystra, impotent in his feet, being a cripple from his mother's womb, who never had walked: the same heard Paul speak: who stedfastly beholding him, and perceiving that he had faith to be healed, said with a loud voice, Stand upright on thy feet. And he leaped and walked."

Acts 19:17-18, 20 relates what happened after the man had been delivered of the evil spirit: "And this was known to all the Jews and Greeks also dwelling at Ephesus; and fear fell on them all, and the name of the Lord Jesus was magnified. And many that believed came, and confessed. . . . So mightily grew the word of God and prevailed."

God has not changed. If these same miracles are not happening now, then the church has changed. It is the will of God for the church to operate in the realm of the supernatural and believe Him to do miracles, signs, and wonders!

You will see from Elsie Lund's story that she lived a daily life that was permeated with the power of the supernatural. It was as natural as breathing because of her trust in God.

ELSIE LUND

When I was asked to be one of the writers for this book, the verse of Scripture in Romans 8:28 came to mind: "And we know that all things work together for good to them that love God, to them who are the called according to his purpose."

We had just completed our Central Canadian District Conference with Brother Garry Tracy as the conference speaker. He is pastor of New Life Pentecostal Church in Bridgeton, Missouri.

One of the many gems he left with us was how the Lord would ask him to do things of which he felt totally inadequate. He would say, "God, I am not able. I have no idea how to approach this task. Help me, Lord." The Lord always helped him.

These words really inspired me. I realized that I am not the only one who has this feeling many times, and surely when Sister Joy Haney asked me to write a chapter for her book I got that exact feeling. I thought to myself: *I am not a writer. I am not able to do this.*

However, God does not ask us to do anything that

He will not help us to do. We can do much more than what we think we can.

> *There hath no temptation taken you but such as is common to man: but God is faithful, who will not suffer you to be tempted above that ye are able; but will with the temptation also make a way of escape, that ye may be able to bear it* (I Corinthians 10:13).

God is always the Master of the situation. God knows that we can stand or do much more than we think we can.

This was demonstrated in Exodus:

> *And he cried unto the LORD; and the LORD shewed him a tree, which when he had cast into the waters, the waters were made sweet: there he made for them a statute and an ordinance, and there he proved them* (Exodus 15:25).

Notice the last part of the verse: *there He proved (or tested) them.*

This is illustrated in the following story:

> I stood once in the test room of a great steel mill. All around me were little partitions and compartments. Steel had been tested to the limit, and marked with figures that showed its breaking point. Some pieces had been twisted until they broke, and the strength of torsion was marked on them. Some had been stretched to the breaking point and their tensile strength indicated. Some had been compressed to the crushing point, and also marked. The master of

the steel mill knew just what these pieces of steel would stand under strain. He knew just what they would bear if placed in the great ship, building, or bridge. He knew this because his testing room revealed it.

It is often so with God's children. God does not want us to be like vases of glass or porcelain. He would have us like these toughened pieces of steel, able to bear twisting and crushing to the uttermost without collapse.

He wants us to be not hothouse plants, but storm-beaten oaks; not sand dunes driven with every gust of wind, but granite rocks withstanding the fiercest storms. To make us such He must needs bring us into His testing room of suffering. Many of us need no other argument than our own experiences to prove that suffering is indeed God's testing room of faith.

—J. H. McC[33]

Yes, this comes through prayer and fasting. Prayer is our lifeline. Prayer is a must. When prayer does not work, fasting will work. God has ordained it thus. Thank God for prayer.

I recall very well the first time I prayed for a purpose as a little girl. I was so afraid of thunder and lightning I would continue to repeat the Lord's Prayer until the storm was over. Dad and Mother had been faithful to teach us the Lord's Prayer from the beginning of our little lives. Our background was Lutheran on both sides of the family as far back as either family has traced. So we are the first generation of Pentecost, believing as the Bible teaches in Acts 2:38. Glory!

Then all three of us children in the family took polio

in 1953 when the epidemic spread. As I lay in the hospital for nine months, I must have prayed the Lord's Prayer hundreds of times. I had no idea how else to pray. The prayer and reading Psalm 23 gave me some comfort. I did not know you could talk to Jesus like a friend and that He could hear you. How wonderful!

After I was discharged from the Sudbury General Hospital, I came home to Dryden, Ontario, and was invited to a healing campaign in Minneapolis, Minnesota. There I was prayed for after the evangelist had preached on repentance. I went to the altar and did what they told me to do. Of course, I did not understand very much yet. Then I joined the healing line where it seemed close to a thousand were lined up one behind the other. This line circled the enormous tent more than once.

With my own eyes I saw many healings, but I will tell you about three miraculous healings. There were two elderly ladies who had goiters that had grown well below their necks on to their chests. The evangelist laid hands on their heads one by one, and I literally saw the skin becoming less and less flabby until finally each neck was back to normal. It was indeed totally miraculous. I had never seen anything like this before. This happened in 1954.

How this increased my faith! I was twenty-one years old but knew little about the Bible. My heart was hungry to know about God. I thought, *If only we had a Pentecostal church in Dryden,* not knowing that the Lord was already at work in hearts to come there.

The third miracle was the one that was right in front of me. The man had Bright's disease, a kidney disease for which there was no cure—only continued blood transfusions. He had been a patient in the Winnipeg General Hospital and they had granted him permission to go! When he returned to the hospital he was healed, so they discharged him for the reason: "Healed by divine intervention." Thus it was documented.

When I was prayed for, it was like an electric current went through my body. My legs were strengthened to normal and my one arm which had been affected the most was strengthened but not totally healed, nor was my one hand. However, God gave me something far more important; Jesus imparted into me a faith and confidence that I needed and have been with me ever since.

The doctor told me I could not teach for one year. That was when I was discharged from the hospital. However, after this experience, I applied for my old position as principal and teacher, and I got it.

One evening as I was at the school, an elderly couple, Brother and Sister Lentz, came and invited me to church. It was in the home of Brother and Sister Kelbert, who had just been in Dryden for a few months. It is now the United Pentecostal Church pastored by Brother and Sister Irvin Wurch. It was in a service in the Kenora, Ontario, United Pentecostal Church that my sister and I first went to the altar and repented. The late Brother W. V. Cooling was the pastor, and Brother John Abbott who pastored the Toronto Church on Greenwood Avenue had come to visit. He was superintendent of the Ontario District, United Pentecostal Church, at that time. That was February 14, 1955.

Following that experience, my life made a total turnabout. I repented of everything I could think of, which took me time. Finally, I accepted by faith that Jesus had forgiven my sins. That was a great joy! I just could not fathom why others could not understand how wonderful the forgiveness of God was. Two weeks later I was baptized in the name of Jesus for the remission of sins and later received the Holy Ghost speaking in other tongues as is commanded in Acts 2:38. If people could only grasp how wonderful this experience is and that they have everything to gain and nothing to lose!

By this time, I surely had the calling to Africa. What a calling! Many tried to discourage me. I was not strong from the polio. I did not consider how I would do it. I knew Jesus called me and I knew He would make a way, and so He did and how He did it! Of course, there were the obstacles. I had met a mining engineer from England. This was before I had the Holy Ghost. He would bring me to church. The church had now grown until the Ukranian Hall had to be rented in Dryden. He would not come to service but would take me there and then come for me after church was over. I had testified to him and wanted so much for him to join me. I was new in the Lord, but I knew this could not go on. I did love the Lord and I had already felt my calling as a missionary in Africa.

One Sunday afternoon topped it all. The pastor's wife asked me to go for a walk, and I remember there was much wisdom in the conversation. Then she quoted II Corinthians 6:14,

> *Be ye not unequally yoked together with unbelievers: for what fellowship hath righteousness with unrighteousness? and what communion hath light with darkness?* (II Corinthians 6:14).

Well, I understood very well what she was trying to tell me, but this was going to be difficult. So the last words between him and me were when he told me, "You love Africa more than me." Yes, it was one of the crossroads in life. I knew I made the right choice and it hurt, but God was in it. The hurt did not last long as I just gave everything to Jesus. "Casting all your care upon him; for he careth for you" (I Peter 5:7).

Then another obstacle came along. It was a young man who was in the church and said that he would go with me to the mission field. Thank God for prayer and fasting. I knew he did not have the calling. I had a dream that he would present me with a parcel which looked sort of like a package unwrapped. Inside was a most beautiful jewelry silver case, shaped like the old-fashioned sugar bowl that stood on four fancy legs. It had a lid with hinges that opened, and inside was the most beautiful red velvet with the rings—both the wedding and the engagement ring—as well as the price tags attached.

The second dream was that he and I were standing at the altar and the pastor had just pronounced us man and wife. The Lord spoke to me and said, "You have married the wrong man!"

It was about two or three AM. I woke up with a start and immediately wrote to him and ended it, not mentioning the dream.

He arrived a few days later and came with the very parcel I had dreamed about exactly. I was so frightened I could not believe what I was seeing. I could not accept or touch anything. He opened it, and when I saw even the same price tags attached, I was beside myself and now had to tell him the dream. This was certainly the end of it.

I have never ever regretted making the choices for Africa and fulfilling my calling. My joy in the Lord has been complete. It pays to pray and fast and ask God to help you in your every choice. He will show you what is right for you. Just let Jesus have His way. I am sure I am the happiest person in the world. I have been so rewarded and so fulfilled in my calling. It has not all been easy. There have been some mighty rocky, scary, dangerous experiences, as well as sad and sorrowful events, though in Jesus "everything will be all right."

In the years that followed, I attended the Apostolic Bible Institute in St. Paul, Minnesota. In 1962, I graduated and in October of the same year was appointed as a missionary to Fassama, Liberia, by the Foreign Missions Board at the General Conference of the United Pentecostal Church International held at Columbus, Ohio.

Sister Pauline Gruse, a great missionary, had resigned from missionary work in Fassama, so there was a need there. I had not heard of Fassama and hardly knew where Liberia was, although I knew it was in Africa and that was all that mattered. I was beside myself with joy and found myself jumping up and down and dancing around my classroom where I was teacher and principal. Of course, this was in the evening after the students had left when I received my letter with my full appointment as a foreign missionary to Liberia, West Africa. I was ecstatic with joy!

I would add here that Sister Pauline Gruse only remained home in America for about one year before she was back in Fassama. So I worked with her for some time before she fell sick and had to leave for Bomi Hills, Liberia, and eventually home. She was indeed a great lady and did a great work. She wrote a book called *I Surrender All*. That is what it takes. I encourage you to read it.

Months before Sister Gruse had become ill, I was praying and found it a must to pray at least an hour a day. I would go to the church as there, no matter what happened, no one would disturb me. They waited until I was finished.

However, for months, as I would return to my home after prayer and walk through the rooms, the impression was so strong, "You will not be here long!" Over and over this happened and always right after prayer. At first and for some time I did not know what this meant. I was so happy teaching, bringing the gospel to the villagers around Fassama, and caring for the sick. We prayed as those brave, courageous mothers delivered their babies in their huts without doctors or nurses. I had to cut the cord on one baby. I bandaged wounds, gave medication for malaria and other sicknesses. Sometimes I was called to the village to take care of wounds. In every case I would always pray first. One time a village chief came rushing into my house carrying a young child, and it seemed like a large part of the village was following him. They were so excited. They walked right into my house, the chief leading the way with the little boy in his arms. I met them on their way into my kitchen. They said, "He has drank kerosene!" So we stood there, right on the spot, and I asked all to bow their heads and we would pray to Jesus. We prayed and the child was healed. All was well. Thank you, Jesus.

Now it was clear to me that the Lord was calling me to Ghana to teach in the Bible college, now known as ACTS: Apostolic Center for Theological Studies, and to visit the various churches on invitation. Most of my missionary years were spent in Ghana, West Africa, and I loved it.

Then after a few years there was again a need in Monrovia, Liberia. Brother and Sister Jim Hall, superintendent of Liberia and president of the Maranatha Bible Institute, were to go on furlough and there was no one to take charge of the Bible school. So Brother Hall put me in charge of MBI until he would return from furlough. Now I was traveling between Liberia and Ghana. Just a few months before Brother and Sister Jim Hall went on furlough in 1989, they received a letter from a pastor that the Lord had told him to have a crusade in the capital city, Monrovia, and that it should be in the month of August that year. Brother Hall answered by suggesting another month because of the heavy rainfall during that time of year. The pastor wrote back and said the Lord said August and to rent the largest stadium for the crusade and that they would take care of the expenses. He said, "As you read this letter, step outside and look at the sky. That will be the confirmation."

Brother and Sister Hall and I were standing by the door of MBI leading to the outside. Brother Hall gave me the letter to read. When I came to the part "Step outside and look at the sky," I thought, *This certainly is different,* but I did. It had been an overcast morning, but when I looked up at the sky the sun was breaking through. So we had the confirmation. God would take care of the weather and He did!

The Kanyon Doe Sports Stadium was rented, which seated thirty-five thousand. Also, the hotel on the stadium grounds was rented. Voice of Pentecost, San Francisco, took care of the cost. Fifty-seven people came. They brought sixty thousand tracts, five thousand posters, six thirty-foot banners to hang across the roads, two twelve-foot swimming pools for baptizing, PA systems, guitars, amplifiers, five thousand pre-recorded cassettes for new converts, and one case of anointing oil.

The results were five hundred baptized in the name of Jesus for the remission of sins and nearly one thousand filled with the Holy Ghost speaking in tongues.

Four months later came the crisis, the beginning of the civil war on December 24, 1989. Tragedy had hit Liberia.

In 1990, we resumed Bible classes as usual, but the fighting was drawing closer to the capital city of Monrovia. We still continued to attend prayer meeting at the headquarters church from 6 to 7 every morning. My apartment was right across the street, which made it convenient for me. Later the time was changed to 7 to 8 AM because of the danger.

For days now they had been announcing on the radio for everyone to evacuate Monrovia immediately! There were planes from several countries coming to help.

The secretary for the Canadian High Commission had been sent from Ghana to Monrovia to warn all Canadian citizens to leave immediately. He came to the office at MBI and asked when I planned to leave. I told him I had been left with a responsibility and that I wished to complete the term which ended in June. It was May. He then told me that I needed to give him the names of my next of kin, which I did.

Then I thought to myself that the Lord brought me here but I had not felt the Lord telling me to go.

In prayer that evening the Lord spoke very clearly. I Peter 5:7: "Casting all your care upon him; for he careth for you." I believed this and did not make preparation to leave. The next morning during devotion I asked for someone to give the first verse of Scripture he or she had on mind. One student jumped up immediately and repeated I Peter 5:7, the very one the Lord had given me the night before. That was a relief and a confirmation.

In the next few days, we completed the courses for the term and gave the final exams on schedule. The exams were graded, recorded, and the financial statements completed. I prepared the books and schedule for the next term, which was to begin in August. There were no banks open at this time or any other businesses. However, when Brother Jim Hall had built the Bible school in Monrovia, he had built a vault into the wall of the office. So the financial statements along with the cash were stored in there. When the Maranatha Bible Institute was reopened several years later, Brother Albert Stewart, being superintendent of UPC of Liberia and president of MBI, found everything intact—nothing missing. Only the money was all mildewed. During these turbulent days, the Lord gave me another verse of Scripture: "in quietness and in confidence shall be your strength." I felt so assured I was going in the right direction.

Then, the last time I stood and turned the key in the door of Maranatha Bible Institute, I felt I had completed my work. As I walked into my apartment across the street, I said, "God, if you want me to stay here I will!" However, in myself I knew it was definitely dangerous. Dead were seen and found so many places.

The next morning, as usual, I went to prayer meeting from 7 AM to 8 AM at the Sinkor church where many of us gathered faithfully. As I walked into the church that morning I saw Sister Quansah, a Ghanaian who was building and pastoring the church in Gbanga. She had fled for her life from the city as had many others. I asked her, "Sister Quansah, would you like to go back to Ghana?" She replied, "Oh yes, but I have no money. I have lost everything. All I have is this little bag under the bench." I asked her if she knew of anyone to make arrangements for us to go back to Ghana. I said, "If you can find someone, I will pay your way." She said, "Oh yes, my friends with whom I am staying live beside the manager for Ghana Airways."

That afternoon of June 11, 1990, she returned to tell me that we were to be on the airfield early the next morning.

The airfield was crowded, and everything total chaos. The counters were all closed; people, people everywhere on the tarmac and all over and only one airplane, Ghana Airways stood there. God made it possible for Sister

Quansah and me, along with the total Ghana Airways staff and others, to fly safely to Ghana. It was the last Ghana Airways flight out for approximately eight years.

God, whose name is Jesus, is so wonderful! I love Him and thank Him for this wonderful salvation. He is so good to me. It is no sacrifice to serve Jesus. It is the greatest privilege that you could ever experience in your life. I would be glad to do it all over again.

Epilogue

WHAT WOULD HE SAY?
If He should come today
And find my hands so full
Of future plans, however fair,
In which my Saviour has no share,
What would He say?

If He should come today
And find my love so cold,
My faith so very weak and dim
I had not even looked for Him,
What would He say?

If He should come today
And find that I had not told
One soul about my Heavenly Friend
Whose blessings all my way attend,
What would He say?

Would I be glad, quite glad?
Remembering that He died for all
And none through me had heard His call,
What would He say?

– AUTHOR UNKNOWN[34]

Let us be glad when He comes! May He find us faithful and working wherever He places us, doing our best to further the gospel of Jesus Christ in the earth, carrying the mantle that has been handed down to us from the early church, and then from generation to generation—handling it with responsibility, doing our part, knowing that it is a privilege to do so!

Guest Authors' Bios

1. NONA FREEMAN

Autobiography of E. L. and Nona Freeman

We met January 25, 1937, a date we celebrated the rest of his life. Love came instantly, though both of us were in such denial about a call to preach and a call to Africa that we did not mention it to each other. God called him before his seventh birthday, and my call came at eleven with the infilling of the Holy Ghost.

I collapsed at college in March that year and was sent home from the hospital with thirty-six hours to live. Death came, but during those thirty minutes of time when my heart did not beat and I did not breathe, I met Jesus face to face. I confessed my disobedience and failures and promised to do His will if He would allow me to come back. He graciously forgave me and sent me back. My life turned around at age twenty. Because of Bug's lack of spirituality I immediately broke our engagement, but Jesus has His own beautiful and exquisite ways of working out His will in human lives.

God later let me know that our marriage agreed with His will, so we were married in August still keeping our secrets. God said I must be still and let Him guide us. Bug's ambition lay in the business world where he had wonderful opportunities, though he had long sought earnestly for the Holy Ghost. When he decided to surrender to God's will and preach, the Spirit came on him wonderfully and he talked in tongues for three days. His preaching (and mine) began in a revival in New Mexico, April 1939. In that revival Jesus told us about Africa, and from that hour, our predominant thoughts concentrated on *going*.

Our deep desire to get to Africa moved us to drive from New Mexico to St. Louis, Missouri, in September 1939 (with great difficulties and without basic necessities) to meet the missionary board. They greeted us with these words, "You look more like you ought to be applying to the TB asylum than the mission field." My husband at 6'2" weighing 125 pounds and I at 5'9" weighing 106 pounds inspired that remark. They felt insulted (rightly so) that with only five months' preaching experience, we would meet them, wanting to be appointed to Africa. This was simple ignorance on our part. However, they gave us good advice: "Don't trade on a missionary call. Work for God, hold meetings, start a new work, go through every door God opens, and come back in three years."

Without resentment we took their advice and tried to meet the board in 1941 and 1942, but they did not have time to see us. By this time, we were pastoring our second church in Louisiana. We asked if we could see them at the conference in 1943. The meeting would begin at 1:00 PM and end about 6:00 PM. If we were there and they had time, they would talk to us. We got to the appointed place at 12:30 PM. When their meeting ended at 6:30 PM, they marched out and said, "Sorry, we don't have time to talk to you this year. Come back next year."

My husband immediately began to encourage me to have the right attitude and not resent anything, promising that when we returned home we would be able to settle everything by prayer. In that all-night prayer meeting, God gave me a verse of Scripture, John 15:16, "Ye have not chosen me, but I have chosen you, and ordained you, that ye should go and bring forth fruit." As I read this to my husband, I started shouting. He had received the same verse and finished reading it: "and that your fruit should remain: that whatsoever ye shall ask of the Father in my name, he may give it you."

At a Louisiana district conference in 1944, the missions director announced that we had a missions call. Our precious friend, George Glass Sr., said, "We love the Freemans and do not want them to leave us, but if they have a call to Africa, we need to send them. Bring your gifts to them and put it in the guitar case!" Everyone began to weep and most of them made several trips to the case to add to that offering. The war raged and America still felt the steely grip of depression, but $3,400 resulted. Three weeks later we received a letter from the board appointing us to Africa if I could pass a doctor's examination on being able to go. At age fifteen a doctor had discovered that I had only one lung, but Jesus gave me a new one just in time so I passed the test. In March 1948, that offering paid the Freemans' fare to Africa on a cargo boat with five children, ages ranging from nine months to six months. No planes to Africa then.

I've written books about our forty-one years of adventure in Africa which prove beyond a shadow of a doubt that the incomparable grace of Jesus is sufficient for every situation. No matter how ugly or desperate the case, He is forever able! One of the most amazing things Jesus did early in our journey was guiding Brother Freeman to visit other African countries by faith and claim them for Jesus. Within a short time of his unofficial visits when he walked over that country and claimed it, someone in America would get a burden for that land and *go*! Then speedily revival's flame would blaze from unexpected quarters. Speaking of revivals, we saw incredible miracles of healing and salvation in the twenty years of tent revivals that we held, often under very challenging conditions all over the country, a rich reward for the small sacrifices we made.

All the missionaries who went before us to Africa were sent to Liberia, a small country on the west coast known as the white man's grave. E. L. Freeman refused to go there. He said, "I am not afraid of the climate, but the rest of that vast continent needs the true gospel!" He carried an immense burden for Africa, and after his twenty-three years in South Africa, the board handed him the whole continent except for the five countries at the top of it (they fall with the Mid-east region). During the time T. F. Tenney served as Foreign Missions Director, for two years he arranged for us to visit, encourage, and try to open other countries. We continued to do this for another eighteen years after Bug's appointment as Regional Field Supervisor (now known as Regional Director). We had many more adventures in Jesus' name trying to open new areas for the preaching of this glorious gospel and saw unusual success in that endeavor.

Somewhere along there, my dearest Bug had to go to St. Louis for a board meeting while I remained in Africa. Jesus visited me in a vision, saying,

The churches in America are in trouble. The affluence of America has robbed them of their trust in me, and they don't even realize it. I'm cutting your missionary work short and sending you back to America. Accept every invitation you get to visit the churches and tell them what you have seen me do and what I can do for them.

When Bug came back, he excitedly told of having the same vision. Shortly after that the board decided we were getting too old to be missionaries. We knew why! We came back to America in 1989 and did what Jesus said to do. During those ten years, there were also some visits overseas. Then my darling got the call to go higher in 1999, but before he left me he told me what to do: "Keep on doing what you're doing and be happy."

A near-fatal accident in Kenya, Africa, in 1973 taught us the beautiful message of praise and worship. It still sustains me at age ninety as my beautiful daughter, Sandra, lives with me and helps me deliver my urgent message to the family of God: "Trust Jesus completely and walk in the liberty and power of the Holy Ghost!"

2. **ELSIE LUND**

The same year that I graduated from the Apostolic Bible Institute, St. Paul, Minnesota, I was appointed as a missionary to Fassama, Liberia, West Africa, by the Foreign Mission Board at the General Conference in Columbus, Ohio, in 1962. I spent the next forty-two years as a missionary for the United Pentecostal Church International and served most of the time in the land of my calling, Africa, serving also six months in Copenhagen, Denmark, and three months in Glasgow, Scotland. These were the happiest years of my life.

Before going to Africa I was a licensed teacher and was a principal and teacher in schools in Ontario, Canada. I also was in charge of a work on an Indian reserve now known as First Nations Wabigoon. I took care of that church, held in a government school building, until I left for Africa. It was a work that I loved very much and that gave me much happiness also.

In Fassama, Liberia, West Africa, I was principal of the mission school, Sunday school superintendent, youth leader, besides caring for the sick and also walking to the various villages teaching the natives the gospel of Jesus Christ.

When I transferred to Accra, Ghana, in 1971, I was an instructor in the College of Bible, now known as ACTS. Also, I was active in the Ladies' Auxiliary program there. I taught in the Bible schools in Abak, Nigeria, Abidjan, Ivory Coast, and then back to Monrovia, Liberia, to the Maranatha Bible Institute, where I was Dean of MBI while missionaries, Brother and Sister Jim Hall, went on deputation. In June of 1990, I evacuated from Liberia due to the civil war. I then remained in Ghana until 1998, when I was appointed for International Teaching Ministries and taught in the Bible schools in the following places: Nairobi, Kenya; Kampala, Uganda; Moshi, Tanzania; Glasgow, Scotland; and Lome, Togo.

It was from Lome, Togo, I was medi-vaced home due to a fall that caused a broken hip and a blood clot.

What a wonderful, God-given privilege it has been to serve under the United Pentecostal Church International. This wonderful God whose name is Jesus has been and is so wonderful! I love Him so much!

3. **VESTA MANGUN**

When Vesta Layne Gibson, daughter of Reverend and Mrs. R. D. Gibson, was a young woman growing up in Angelina County, Texas, she heard an illustrious evangelist preach in her hometown. His name was Gerald Archie Mangun, and after this meeting in February 1943, they married that same year in the fall.

They began action immediately, increasing their evangelistic work all over America until they came to Alexandria, Louisiana, in 1950 to assume the pastorate of a congregation of thirty-five people. Their only son, Anthony, was five months old at this time.

Vesta Mangun was very active standing alongside her husband in the teaching ministry of the church, advancing his evangelistic programs through her example of prayer, fasting, and praise. In addition to this, she is an anointed vocalist and musician.

During the Manguns' tenure in Alexandria, there have been five building programs related to the church, and the entire city has been blitzed six times with the Pentecostals' message.

Twenty-four-hour prayer programs were begun with only thirty to forty members. The week of prayer was every quarter until 1972, when they began around-the-clock prayer and fasting.

Vesta Mangun has been and is still a featured speaker at the "Because of the Times" conference, which began in 1983, and also has been a well-known speaker at women's conferences, prayer conferences, and camp meetings all over America for many years.

She is still a vital force in the church where her husband serves as the bishop of *The Pentecostals of Alexandria*, with their son, Anthony, who is senior pastor, along with his talented wife, Mickey.

Someone close to her wrote the following about her:

> *A piece of life devoted to God. Israel in captivity had Esther. In the time of battle, they had Deborah. In the Exodus, they had Miriam. The church today in unsettling, uncharted waters has Vesta Layne Mangun. As a woman of the times, anchored to the Rock, she shines light on the vision and purpose of Jesus Christ. Souls! Souls! Souls! She charges us to carry out His will and then equips us with the principles of prayer and discipleship. Our course is made clear. The decision is ours to make. The clock is ticking. The time is now. The battle call has sounded. Regardless of your choice, to run or remain in place, your life will never be the same.*

4. **NILAH MEAN**

Eunilah Mean, an ordained minister with the UPCI, began her fruitful ministry when her pastor in Granite City, Illinois, asked her to preach a revival meeting in his place. She received permission to leave her job for the meeting and never went back. From that beginning, she felt she had found the true niche for her life.

The daughter of Llewellyn and Rose Rutledge, Nilah, as she is known, felt the call of God upon her life when just a young child living in Roodhouse, Illinois. The family attended a Pentecostal revival in White Hall, Illinois, and Nilah was the first to go to the altar. She immediately set up her place of prayer, an old tree stump near her home. It was while she faithfully prayed that she felt the call of God deeper and deeper in her spirit.

The evangelistic field is where Nilah spent many years. One of her early converts was a former Carmelite nun, Sister Charlotte, who was equally passionate regarding the work of God. The two of them evangelized together for about fourteen years.

Nilah and Charlotte were invited to preach the first camp meeting in Nova Scotia in 1952. Afterwards they teamed up with the Lewis DeMerchant family and John Mean, also an evangelist, to preach the first revival meetings in the province, returning in 1953 and 1954. During these times of working for the Lord, John and Nilah Mean were falling in love. They married and evangelized for two years before returning to Nova Scotia to start their first church in Amherst. They soon felt the call back to Halifax to pastor a church there. Shortly thereafter Nilah felt led to start a work in Dartmouth, across the harbor from Halifax. As her husband continued to pastor in Halifax, Nilah started the work in Dartmouth and served as pastor for twenty-eight years.

A faithful servant of the Lord during her more than sixty years of ministry, Nilah turned her pastoral duties over to another minister in 2005, but she continues to serve in the role of senior pastor.

John and Nilah Mean are the parents of four children.

5. **BOBBYE WENDELL**

Bobbye Wendell is an ordained minister with the United Pentecostal Church International. She and her husband were appointed as founding missionaries to Ethiopia in 1966, where they saw the Lord perform many miracles. After the passing of her husband, Sister Wendell served as Dean of Women and Missions instructor at Gateway College of Evangelism. She spent more than two years of resident missionary work in Israel.

Upon appointment to Kenya in the late 1970s, she served as administrator and instructor in the Bible school, as ladies ministries coordinator, and as an evangelist. She has traveled extensively, having visited and preached in more than twenty-five countries for over forty-six years. When she is not at her residence of many years in Oil City, Louisiana, Sister Wendell travels nationally and internationally as a speaker at women's conferences. She has been blessed with four children, nine grandchildren, and seven great-grandchildren.

Notes

[1]Knight, Walter B., *Knight's Treasury of Illustrations,* (Eerdmans Publishing Co., Grand Rapids, MI: 1963), p. 267.

[2]Urshan, Andrew D., *Prayer: The Supreme Need of the Hour,* (Apostolic Book Publishers, Portland OR: 1981), p. 96.

[3]Johnson, Joseph S., compiled by, *A Field of Diamonds*, (Broadman Press, Nashville, TN: 1974), p. 71.

[4]*Ibid.*

[5]Urshan, p. 29.

[6]Johnson, p. 72.

[7]*Ibid.,* p. 28.

[8]*Ibid.,* p. 121.

[9]Howell, Clinton T., compiled by, *Lines to Live By,* (Thomas Nelson Inc., Nashville, TN: 1972), p. 18.

[10]Johnson, p. 114.

[11]Knight, p. 443.

[12]*Ibid.,* p. 114.

[13]*Ibid.,* p. 114.

[14]*Ibid.,* p. 115.

[15]Johnson, p. 78.

[16]Howell, p. 180.

[17]Johnson, p. 82.

[18]*Ibid.,* p. 55.

[19]Howell, p. 29.

[20]*Ibid.,* p. 102.

[21]*Ibid.,* p. 172.

[22]Johnson, p. 31.

[23]Howell, p. 112.

[24]Tan, Paul Lee, *Encyclopedia of 7700 Illustrations,* (Assurance Publishers, Rockville, MD: 1979), 3111.

[25]*Ibid.,* 3110.

[26]Johnson, p. 71.

[27]*Tan,* 3208.

[28]Howell, p. 109.

[29]*Ibid.,* p. 106.

[30]*Ibid.,* p. 107.

[31]*Ibid.,* pp. 180-181.

[32]Johnson, p. 122.

[33]Cowman, Mrs. Charles E., *Streams in the Desert, Volume One,* (Zondervan Publishing House, Grand Rapids, MI), August 28, pp. 253-254.

[34]Tan, 7235.